THE

Koehler Method

OF

UTILITY DOG TRAINING

"Apple", (left) owned by Bob Lyons, and "Kenna" owned by Charles Hornback. These Irish Setters were the top pair in Utility work in both the Southern California Top Dogs competition and in the California North-South playoffs. Kenna went on to win the Western Regional Super Dog title. These dogs were trained by their owners while enrolled in classes sponsored by the Orange Empire Dog Club, instructed by the author. They represented the De Anza Dog Obedience Club during competition.

THE
Koehler Method
OF
UTILITY
DOG
TRAINING

William R. Koehler

ILLUSTRATED

Second Edition

HOWELL BOOK HOUSE

Also by William R. Koehler

The Koehler Method of Dog Training
The Koehler Method of Guard Dog Training
The Koehler Method of Open Obedience for Ring, Home and Field (with Retrieving)
The Koehler Method of Training Tracking Dogs

Howell Book House
A Simon & Schuster Macmillan Company
1633 Broadway
New York, NY 10019

Library of Congress Cataloging-in-Publication Data
Koehler, William R.
    The Koehler method of utility dog training / by William R. Koehler.
    —2nd ed.
        p. cm.
    ISBN 0-87605-785-7
    1. Dogs—Obedience trials—Utility classes. 2. Dogs—Training.
    I. Title.
    SF425.7.K63   1991
636.7′0886—dc20   91-9344
                                                        CIP

10 9 8 7 6 5 4 3

Printed in the United States of America

To the memory of
Ethel "Peggy" Reynolds

Contents

Acknowledgments

MY THANKS to all of you who supplied the valuable feedback on the innovations introduced in our classes. To the friends who aided in the photography, my gratitude for your cooperation and patience.

William R. Koehler

Foreword

to the First Edition

To THOUSANDS of obedience enthusiasts all across the United States and Canada, only a few trainers are considered preeminent in the field. And of these William R. Koehler is in a class by himself.

William Koehler's brilliant career as teacher and trainer spans over three decades and encompasses virtually every type of dog training imaginable. During World War II he was an instructor in the U.S. Army K-9 Corps, training men and dogs and also leading special training projects. Since the war he held the post of Training Director for the Orange Empire Dog Club, the largest dog club in the world.

It was in his capacity for more than twenty years as Chief Trainer for the Walt Disney Studios that William Koehler's singular talents came to national attention. For it was he who trained the "stars" of *Big Red*, *The Shaggy Dog*, *The Ugly Dachshund*, *The Swiss Family Robinson*, *The Incredible Journey* and many other celebrated animal actors. Five Koehler pupils won the American Humane Association's coveted Patsy

Award for outstanding performances in movies and television.

But the greatest testimonial to William Koehler's ability is the success of his methods with the tens of thousands of happy, well-adjusted dogs that have been trained by them. These include field dogs, guard dogs and chronic "problem" dogs once thought antisocial beyond help.

To his estimable talent as a dog trainer, William Koehler adds the happy faculty of easily communicating with people, in person and in writing. His first book, *The Koehler Method of Dog Training*, is still a bestseller fifteen years after initial publication, and at this writing has gone back to press twenty times!

The Koehler Method of Guard Dog Training, his second book, is the definitive work in the field and was named Best Dog Book of 1967 by the Dog Writers Association of America. With his third book, *The Koehler Method of Open Obedience for Ring, Home and Field*, William Koehler showed how to get more out of a dog as a companion, an obedience competitor and a gun dog. It is one of the few books that can guarantee results from the use of its proven methods.

The Koehler Method of Utility Dog Training follows the tradition of excellence readers have come to expect. Now you can prepare your dog and yourself for advanced obedience in the incomparable Koehler manner.

Always a logical, no-nonsense trainer, William Koehler may occasionally surprise you by what he says, but his methods work. The demand for his books, personal appearances and Koehler seminars, and the size of his devoted following, have distinguished him as one of the most gifted dog trainers of all time.

It is with great pleasure and pride that we present to the obedience fancy William Koehler's newest book—*The Koehler Method of Utility Dog Training*.

ELSWORTH HOWELL
Publisher

Prologue

"THERE IS an infinite number of ways in which a good dog can fail in Utility work."

This statement, made by an experienced trainer and exhibitor, reflects realism, not pessimism. Indeed, it sometimes appears that weird complications come from the realm of the occult to put a single twist in the path of a dog who otherwise performs superbly.

May this book help to protect you and your dog from the "Utility Gremlins."

1

Read It and Walk It

A TECHNICAL BOOK that advocates specific actions will inevitably cause the reader to question the need and justification for those actions. While it is true that such assurance might best be understood at the time of the reader's questions, it is not practical to interrupt the continuity of instruction for philosophical discourses. But by some means the reader must be enabled to proceed with confidence, knowing that understanding will grow and the justification will appear as each step of the process is completed.

Read this book completely before you start your Utility training. Then, before you involve your dog, **walk through it.** Walk through it in the way one should walk through any instructions that cannot be kept in hand while one works. If you will walk through it in a ring setup, you will be better able to understand and remember positions and actions. When you have made most of the moves without a dog, the sensory experience will make your moves with your dog more accurate and confident.

THE NEED FOR POSITIVE RETRIEVING

Two of the Utility exercises require a dog to retrieve. One component of another exercise depends on retrieving as a motivation. All references to retrieving in this book are based on the assumption that the reader has a positively motivated retriever and not one of the *fun and games* kind. Warning! If you have a dog who is a *natural* or *fun* retriever and you find that he doesn't feel natural or like playing the *game,* don't try to suddenly surprise him with a correction. While force-retrieving is easily taught with a logically structured program, it can be unfair when it is attempted in an unstructured, haphazard way. This book deals with how to use positive retrieving, not how to teach it, a subject that should be covered during Open work.

THE LIGHT LINE

At all levels of obedience training, the author advocates that the transition from control with the leash, longe or checkcord be made by the use of a light, almost invisible line that will be gradually shortened as the dog's reliability on a given exercise grows. Occasionally, an amateur trainer protests that it is awkward to work a dog that is dragging a line. Awkward? Not nearly so awkward as the unfortunate situation that finds a slow-footed handler attempting to head off a dog who is trying to avoid his responsibility or to outrun a correction.

As to the dog who "just won't retrieve if he's dragging a line," such an excuse could not possibly apply to a properly motivated retriever, even if the line were snagged on grass or weeds. Use the line as a step to off-leash control on any exercise where the dog could possibly dodge his responsibilities. Don't gamble. Use the light line and gradually shorten it. Remove the last few feet only when he shows you that his contention is a thing of the past.

**Some useful lines for Utility training. They are (from top) a fif-
teen-foot longe, a seventy-foot check cord, a light line and tab.**

TIME SCHEDULES

It is true that trainers and dogs vary greatly in their foundations and abilities and that no rigid time schedules could apply to all of them. However, trainers who use this book need something in the way of reasonable increments and goals.

The schedule of successful Utility classes would be a reasonable approximation of time needs. The author's Utility courses are of twelve to fourteen weeks' duration. Each class is about ninety minutes long.

It is important to remember that the time-consuming complexities of some Utility exercises will not permit any dog or handler to work on all of the exercises in one period during the early stages of training. It could normally require an hour to successfully introduce your dog to the components of the Directed Jump and the start of the Signal exercise. In another period, the first work on Scent Discrimination might only leave time for the Moving Stand and Examination and a bit of practice on the Signal exercise. The Directed Retrieve, at some levels, can also require most of an average training period. These demands and the limitations they impose are reflected in the Utility classes which in early stages allow time to work only three or four dogs as demonstrators on the complex exercises.

The foregoing facts should indicate that any individual trainer or class instructor who uses this book as a text must create a flexible schedule that will allow for the complexity of some of the exercises and the varied abilities of handlers and dogs.

As previously stated, the proven class schedule of twelve to fourteen weeks should indicate that a student who obtains equal instruction from a book only could require as much as sixteen weeks to achieve the same goals. Take each step in the order it is given, and hold to each level until your dog is past contention before going to the next progression. **The trainer who tries to abridge or sneak around contention is the one who later pays a penalty because of "goofing gaps."** Success does beget success—particularly in dog training.

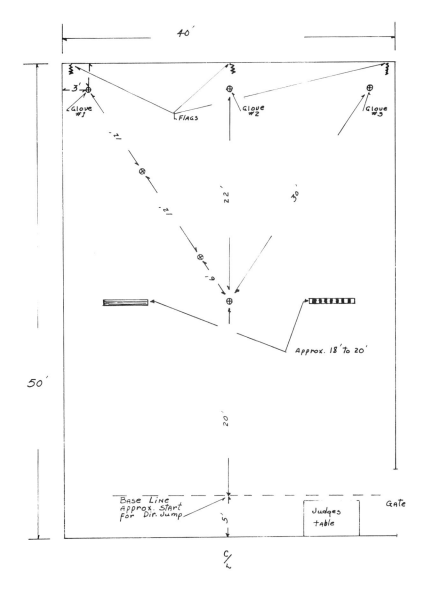

A typical plan of the Utility ring at an obedience trial.

Eventually the exercises will be practiced and polished in the order in which they will be performed in a trial, but good judgment would suggest that early training should follow an order of greatest clarity for the dog. For example: during the learning stages, the Scent Discrimination and Directed Retrieve, both of which involve retrieving, and the Directed Jump which employs retrieving as a motivation, should be separated in each work session by exercises or components that do not relate to retrieving. In the cases of some dogs and trainers, it could well be that hours or even days should separate the start of work on such exercises as the Directed Retrieve and the Directed Jump in order to avoid confusion. Helpful, but not necessarily sufficient, is the rule of thumb that a dog should be trained to a point of success on the first level of an exercise before he's introduced to the first level of another exercise that's at all similar in pattern.

Set up each training increment with consideration of how it must appear to your dog in relation to what he has just been doing. Have your objectives and a plan of action firmly in mind when you start a session so that you will present a positive, not a probing, edge to your dog. Be cheered by the fact that, as your dog learns more of each exercise, the problems of order become fewer.

AKC GENERAL REGULATIONS FOR THE UTILITY CLASS

Section 1. **Utility A Class.** The Utility A class shall be for those dogs that have won the C.D.X. title, but have not won the U.D. title. Obedience Judges or persons who have owned, trained or exhibited a dog that has earned an O.T.Ch. may not enter or handle dogs in this class. Each dog must be handled by its owner or by a member of the owner's immediate family. Owners may enter more than one dog in this class.

Section 2. **Utility B Class.** The Utility B class shall be for dogs that have won the title C.D.X. or U.D. Dogs in this class may be handled by the owner or any other person and owners may enter more than one dog in this class. No dog may be entered in both Utility A and Utility B classes at any one trial.

Section 3. **Utility Exercises and Scores.** The exercises, maximum scores and order of judging in the Utility classes are:

1. Signal Exercise .... 40 points
2. Scent Discrimination
   Article No. 1 .... 30 points
3. Scent Discrimination
   Article No. 2 .... 30 points
4. Directed Retrieve .... 30 points
5. Moving Stand and Examination.......... 30 points
6. Directed Jumping .... 40 points
   Maximum Total Score .... 200 points

Section 4. **U.D. Title.** The American Kennel Club will issue a Utility Dog certificate for each registered dog, and will permit the use of the letters "U.D." after the name of each dog that has been certified by three different Judges of Obedience Trials to have received Qualifying scores in Utility classes at three Licensed or Member Obedience Trials in each of which three or more dogs actually competed in the Utility class or classes, except that at breed club specialties and at any trial in Puerto Rico, Hawaii or Alaska, qualifying scores will be credited towards the title, provided the sum total of dogs that actually competed in all of the regular obedience classes is not less than six.

Swing your left hand out sharply against the leash as you step off on the left foot.

2

The Signal Exercise

In NOVICE WORK your dog's quality of attention meant primarily that he heard and responded to your verbal commands and remembered to hold on his stay-exercises regardless of the conditions around him. In Open work, all of the exercises were off-leash, which demanded that your dog be more aware of your commands and his own responsibilities. However, in both Novice and Open work attention would permit a dog to be momentarily distracted. He could look around while doing the exercises as long as he remembered his responsibility to the last command and was prepared to hear and respond to any subsequent commands. In Utility work, attention requires something entirely different. Specifically, the **Signal exercise** demands not only awareness and concentration: it demands focus, visual focus. If a dog is not watching during the few seconds to which a judge would limit a complete response to his order for a hand signal, he will blow the exercise.

It is this lack of constant focus that causes most failures on the **Signal exercise.** Your dog **must** watch you regardless of distractions.

Remember, it should be one of our objectives and a constant concern as we teach the signals to instill the quality of *focus* in the dog.

The basic mechanics that most trainers use to teach the **Signal exercise** are quite simple and logical. Actually, with the exception of sitting from the down position, a dog at the level of Open work has performed in response to verbal commands all of the actions that compose the exercise. Because of this previous experience, the components can be combined and practiced as a complete pattern much sooner than is true of other multi-faceted exercises. However, it remains advisable to solidly associate each component with the related signal before combining them; otherwise praise and correction might be jammed too close together for clarity. Deal with the components in the order they occur in the exercise.

HEEL SIGNAL

Level 1—Objective: To start heeling promptly on signal.

Each time you started a **Heel exercise** by stepping out with your left foot in unison with your verbal command, you gave your dog somewhat of a signal. The movement of your left leg has come to mean **Heel,** just as leaving a dog by stepping out on the right foot in coordination with a verbal command has come to mean **Stay.**

Because of these leg-signals you've been using, the change to signal only can be easily made. Continue to use your verbal command for a few more training periods as you start out on the left foot with a long, emphatic step. Hold the leash in your right hand with a bit less slack than usual. In precise unison with your verbal command, swing your left arm straight ahead and **into the leash** as you step out. Because of the emphasis of your swing, your hand will pass by your dog's head and into the leash, strongly associating it with your start. Obviously you must bend a little so your swing contacts the leash if you are working with a small dog, just as you would bend to signal him after he's trained. There's nothing compromising about adjusting so he can see the signal. He wouldn't be getting a fair signal if it were to pass two feet over his head. There are handlers who like to swing their Heel signals along the left side of their dog's head and across his eyes in order to **corral** his attention. Such a gesture cannot take advantage of contact with the leash during the training stage, and even with a trained dog has some disadvantages, as any small woman with a Saint Bernard could tell you. Swing it out along his right side and into the leash.

You can be sure that a dozen good starts during each of two periods will prepare a dog to work on the Heel signal alone. Then you can eliminate the voice command, but continue to be emphatic with your arm and leg movement. When he's responding promptly, increase the slack in the leash so that it hangs below the swing of your signal. Give him nothing to hear or feel so that he will have to depend on your signal to tell him of your start. This is the point where you will bid for his undivided attention, so be doubly sure to give no cue other than your signal, and, with your leash grip locked tightly to your body, start out fast. If he happened to be looking away, he will experience a solid jolt as your body slams into the slack, and you will give him the first of many experiences that will convince him that he must watch for your signals in order to avoid discomfort.

Level 2—Objective: Reliable response around distractions.

Arrange for some fair and realistic distractions to occur off to your dog's left, so that you can time your starts to when he looks away from you. It is now time to whet his attention to where he will take the dropping of a chair, growls or barks, or any of the many surprises that occur at trials as a reason to watch for your signal.

Avoid like a plague the moronic practice of delaying your signal until the dog looks your way. Many compromising souls fail to realize that a judge means *now* when he orders a signal. Could it actually be that such a person believes that his dog will acquire attentiveness if he delays his signal until the dog looks in the right direction?

Give your signal and start fast.

A good distraction and a good time to start.

Stop walking and twist around to bring your right hand against the dog's chest as shown.

The **Heel exercise,** with the opportunity for immediate correction it provides, is one of the best means of making a dog attentive to signals. Use distractions. Communicate only with signal. Start abnormally fast until you feel your dog is distraction-proof. Practice the exercise only on leash until you are told to do differently.

STAND AND STAY SIGNALS

Level 1—Objective: To stop quickly in a standing position on signal and **Stay** on a second signal.

In the ring, the order to **Stand Your Dog** will be given after your dog has started on signal and has performed a complete pattern of heeling and turns according to usual ring procedure. There are two good reasons why you should work on the **Stand and Stay** in close combination with the preliminary of the full pattern of heeling and turns, as it will be performed in the ring, instead of signaling the dog to **Heel** and then almost immediately signaling him to **Stand:** (1) The lesson will be preceded by the feeling of success that will come from doing the **Heeling Pattern** that the dog knows so well. (2) You and your dog will both get the balance and feel of doing the component after the full ring preliminary.

End the **Heeling Pattern** by introducing your dog to the stand-from-a-walk-signal. Give him a command to **Stand** and simultaneously stop walking, and twist to bring your right hand against his chest as shown on page 28. Why the right hand?

Because, until he's had a bit of experience stopping in a standing position, a dog will often start to sit automatically when he stops at **Heel.** Naturally, the left hand is in the best position to stop the dog's descent or to correct him back to a **Stand** as you did in **Novice work,** while the right hand on his chest stops the forward motion. When he's standing firmly, the left hand can be used to stroke his back while you praise him. Now face back to the front so your left hand, fingers spread, can give the **Stay** signal as you step out on the right foot to leave the dog. Face him from a leash-length away. After a half

Dogs can be good distractions for each other when they are being taught signals.

minute or so, return and praise him for the **Stay** part of the exercise. Bear in mind that he'll need lots of practice in waiting attentively for your signals in the ring. It will be good to let him feel success on the **Stand** and **Stay** components before you add the other signals.

Level 2—Objective: Reliable response around distractions.

Work carefully on the above until your dog is responding reliably and smoothly to your signals. Then give him experience around distractions. Again, be sure not to delay your signals until he is looking at you. Give him a good **Signal** and correct him if he misses it. He'll learn to watch you.

DROP SIGNAL

Level 1—Objective: To **Drop** from a standing position.

It is in teaching the **Drop signal** that many over-confident trainers do costly damage to a dog's performance. They are the ones who protest, "But why do I want to work him at a leash-length when he's been dropping on the **Recall** in **Open**?" There are several answers to that question. If he were dropped on a verbal command in the ring, as the laws of percentages would say he should have been, his name called attention to the command that would follow. Even if you went against percentages and used a signal to drop him, he would probably be looking at you because he was coming toward you in the **Recall Pattern** that had been deeply ingrained since **Novice work.** Both of these favorable premises are radically different from a situation in which the dog is standing motionless and receptive to the distractions around him. **A dog doesn't look where he's going when he's motionless!**

Work closely until your dog is distraction-proof, so you won't be tempted to wait for his attention. Never cue with a

Work close when you start teaching the drop signal so you can prevent any forward movement.

foot-stomp, or resort to one of the other asinine practices that louse up good dogs.

Work on the **Drop signal** as a separate component for a while. Place the dog on a **Stand** and face him from a step away.

If you are right-handed, hold the leash in your left hand. Now, just as though you were reviewing the introduction to the Drop on Recall, give a verbal command, raise your signal hand, associate a verbal command and step in to bring the hand down to grasp the leash close to the collar and follow through in a way that makes it necessary for the dog to drop. Your step-in should place your foot and leg in such a way that the dog cannot move toward you so much as an inch. If he dropped before your action could tighten the leash, as he probably did, he felt not the slightest discomfort. Move your signal hand from the leash to the dog's head in an appreciative pat. Circle around behind him as you would on a **Stay.** Remember: he must do more than respond to a signal. He must wait attentively for the next one. Break him out of the position with a **Heel** command. Because of previous experience in Open work, five or six of these short patterns should be plenty to convince him that your upraised hand means **Drop.** An equal number of these patterns during each of two daily periods for a week is generally sufficient to prepare him for the challenge of distractions.

Level 2—Objective: Reliability around distractions.

In the name of good scores and saved entry fees, it's now time to make a concentrated effort to convince your dog that distractions will be no excuse for him to miss your signal. Make a set-up like the one shown on page 41, and remember why you made it. Again, don't delay a signal because your dog isn't looking at you. Simply work the pattern. Any discomfort he experiences will be brought on by himself. He can stay ahead of your mechanics by merely watching you.

Work hard on this close pattern each day until he takes all reasonable distractions as reasons to be attentive. By this time he should be dropping the moment your hand goes up and before it can flash down to grab the leash. When you are convinced of his reliability, give the **Drop signal** without the step-in. Be ready to show him you'll condone no slow responses. If he hesitates, lunge in and show him he shouldn't have waited.

Caution! If he waits until you almost get to him, then drops before the leash can tighten, take a short, two-handed grip on the leash, snug it upward without lifting him, and jerk back downward. A bit awkward, yes; but better than letting him think he can get by with his little game. If he waits for it, let him have it. Regulations say he must drop on your signal—not after you move toward him. Anytime you move toward him from now on, it should be for a correction, not for a cue.

When he's dropping in his tracks on signal around distractions, work for the same response from a leash length distance. Stay at this distance until you've added all components to this length pattern.

SIT SIGNAL

Level 1—Objective: To sit from a down position on signal.

Because a dog is not required to sit from a down position prior to the Utility level, it is necessary to do a bit more "teaching" than is needed on the other components of the **Signal exercise.**

To begin the session, place your dog on a **Down-Stay** and face him from one big step away. With your signal hand hanging at your side, use the other hand to hold the leash without slack. The choice of hands is yours to make.

Command "Joe, Sit," as you swing your hand forward and up into the leash and take a step forward to prevent the dog from coming toward you. Give him practice in waiting as you move around him to end the action just as you did on the **Drop** component. In most respects the time increments and progressions of distance will be very similar to those described for use on the **Drop signal.**

34

Swing your hand forward and up into the leash as you take a giant step toward the dog.

35

Level 2—Objective: Reliability around distractions.

Start using your distractions at the point where the dog has learned and is responding to your **Sit signal** from a step away.

Gradually work out to a leash length from the dog, and continue at that distance until it's time to combine the components.

RECALL SIGNAL

Objective: To recall reliably on signal under distracting conditions.

Your dog has been doing the **Recall** and **Finish** since Novice days, so associating the actions with your signals will be easy.

First, decide which hand you will use to give the **Recall signal.** Many good handlers believe that there is less chance for confusion if at least one of the signals, which are given as you face the dog, is given with other than the usual hand. Others are so much more adept in the use of one hand than the other that dexterity governs their choice.

Leave your dog on the **Sit-Stay** and face him from a leash length away. Hold the leash rather snug and level with the hand of your choice. As you give a verbal **Recall command,** start a "beckoning signal" that extends your hand out sideways from your shoulder and then sweep it around to grab the leash as far out in front as you can reach. That hand should pull the leash toward you as it comes back to end up against your chest. The motion is much the same as you used to handle the leash when you taught the **Novice Recall.** Let your hands hang in a neutral position as the dog sits before you.

Your dog will soon take that big sweeping motion that brings in the leash as a signal to come in before the collar can tighten.

36

He won't try to inch toward you if you move toward him first.

FINISH SIGNAL

Your dog has long performed the **Recall** and **Finish** in combination, so, when he comes in to sit in front of you, you can add the **Finish** signal to your usual verbal command and mechanics.

Necessarily, the hand you will use to signal for a **Finish** will be determined by the way the dog "finishes" to your left side. Whichever hand you use, be sure that it reaches out, in association with your command, to grasp the leash and sweeps around to move the dog to his final position in a smooth and logical manner. Teach and use a full and eloquent signal! The little finger spiral, or twitch, that a hot-dogging handler uses, could be missed if his dog were to blink.

Your dog will learn in one or two sessions to finish on a signal without your verbal command. If he shouldn't respond, that signaling hand on the leash will move him.

Don't try the signal off-leash until you are told to do so.

COMBINING THE COMPONENTS OF THE SIGNAL EXERCISE

You taught the components separately so that praise and correction could be given with the utmost clarity. Your dog now understands each part and what it is that he does right or wrong. Now you can practice all of the components in the regulation sequence, but, until you've worked the full pattern around far more distracting sights, smells and sounds than your dog would normally encounter, work only on your six-foot training leash.

Set up a variety of conditions in your ring, such as are shown on page 26. Start and finish your heeling pattern with distractions a few feet on each side of you. As was said before, the action of heeling will demand his attention as you move along. It is as he waits for the next signal that his attention is most apt to stray. Be ready to convince him that he had better see your signal.

Have an experienced or carefully instructed person run

Lay out the light line and attach it as explained in the text.

you through the signal exercise in this on-leash pattern. He should observe whether you signal in quick response to his instruction or wait for the dog to look at you. Also, if he's qualified, have your helper check the clarity of your signals from the dog's level and viewpoint.

When you are responding to the orders of the "judge" properly, and your dog is responding to your signals regardless of the distractions around him, you can lengthen the working distance gradually by using a longe line. At this point, occasionally do the complete **Signal exercise** in strange non-ring situations. You might luck into some good distractions, so be ready to praise and correct in these situations.

Only when your dog seems to be absolutely reliable at a longe length of fifteen feet is it safe to lengthen the distance through use of a light line and tab as illustrated on page 39. As you should know, the line should be so light that the dog will hardly feel the difference when, **much later, it is gradually cut back in length and finally removed.** The light line is very strong and will prevent a smart-alecky dog from successfully avoiding a correction should he have missed your signal due to his inattentiveness. The tab, shown on page 17, is to give you a good handle after you've worked your way down the line to correct him.

Happily, the good foundation you built when working close should make it unnecessary for you to run in for many corrections when working at greater distances; but the line and tab will convince the dog that you still hold the high cards.

There is a truth that every dog trainer should learn during basic work:

No dog—in fact, no mathematician—can estimate his chances of successfully running to avoid correction when he's on a light line if he doesn't know where the end of that line is. If the consequences of his attempts to run are memorably discomforting, a dog comes to remember the **line** and not measure the length of it.

A good technique is to have the line laid out in such a way that you can casually attach it to the tab, which should be already in place on the collar before you leave the dog on the **Stand-Stay** part of the exercises. **Now, give your signals from the free**

Use your imagination to work with your dog in as many different types of distractions as possible.

41

end of the line. There is no way he can avoid a correction if you should have to move in to solve a problem.

Reduce the length of the line gradually and only when you feel your dog is past any thoughts of trying to avoid a correction. Even four or five feet of line stretched in front of him will eventually have a strong influence. This carry-over from the full length of line will be true even when only the tab is left on to remind him that you still have a handle to grab. **Your dog's performance will tell you when even the "handle" can be removed.**

May your long efforts bring you to the time when the sights, sounds and smells of the ring will remind your dog to watch for your signal.

AKC REGULATIONS FOR
THE SIGNAL EXERCISE

Section 5. **Signal Exercise.** The principal features of this exercise are the ability of dog and handler to work as a team while heeling, and the dog's correct responses to the signals to Stand, Stay, Drop, Sit and Come.

Orders are the same as in Heel on Leash and Figure Eight, with the additions of "Stand your dog," which shall be given only when dog and handler are walking at normal pace, and "Leave your dog." The Judge must use signals for directing the handler to signal the dog to Drop, to Sit and to Come, in that sequence, and to Finish.

Heeling in the Signal Exercise shall be done in the same manner as in Heel Free, except that throughout the entire exercise the handler shall use signals only and must not speak to his dog at any time. On order from the Judge, "Forward," the handler may signal his dog to walk at heel, and on specific order from the Judge in each case, shall execute a "Left turn," "Right turn," "About turn," "Halt," "Slow," "Normal" and "Fast." These orders may be given in any sequence and may be repeated as necessary, but the Judge shall attempt to standardize the heeling pattern for all dogs in the class.

On order from the Judge, and while the dog is walking at heel, the handler shall signal his dog to Stand in the Heel position near one end of the ring. On further order, "Leave your dog," the handler shall signal his dog to Stay, go to the other end of the ring and turn to face his dog. On separate and specific signals from the Judge, the handler shall give his signals to Drop, to Sit, to Come and to Finish as in the Novice Recall. During the heeling part of this exercise the handler may not give any signal except when a command or signal is permitted in the Heeling exercises.

Section 6. **Signal Exercise, Scoring.** A dog that fails, on a single signal from the handler, to Stand or remain standing where left, or to Drop, or to Sit and Stay, or to Come, or that receives a command or audible signal from the handler to do any of these parts of the exercise, shall be scored zero.

Minor or substantial deductions depending on the specific circumstances in each case, shall be made for a dog that walks forward on the Stand, Drop or Sit portions of the exercise.

A substantial deduction shall be made for any audible command during the Heeling or Finish portions of the exercise.

All the penalties listed under the Heel on Leash and Figure Eight and the Novice Recall exercises shall apply.

3

Scent Discrimination

REVIEW THE CONCEPT you gained from watching dogs work in the Utility ring. It will lend logic and purpose to your actions as you employ the following instructions.

SCENT ARTICLES

You might recall seeing quite a variety in the form and size of the articles used. Regulations state:

> The articles shall be provided by the handler and these shall consist of two sets, each comprised of five identical articles not more than six inches in length, which may be items of everyday use. One set shall be made entirely of rigid metal, and one of leather of such design that nothing but leather is visible except for the minimum amount of thread necessary to hold the article together.

Although each article must be identical to others of the same material, the leather and metal can differ from each other

44

in form. This permits the use of such common objects as fruit jar rings and simple rolls of leather. However, there is a definite advantage in using articles such as shown on page 46. They stand above the level of stubble found occasionally in rings, and the dog that grabs one runs little chance of a jabbed nostril and a sneezing spell.

These articles have two, three or four crossbars. Some prefer four bars because it puts two bars off the ground for the dog to smell. Others point out that the article that holds only one bar off the ground is actually easier to seize for a big dog like a St. Bernard or a flat-faced dog such as a Pug. Regardless of the article's construction, it should not be difficult for your dog to properly pick up and hold. One and one-half inches high for a Toy and two and one-half inches for a large dog are examples of practical sizes.

It's advisable to decide on the kind of articles you would like to use in trials and begin your training with them.

Level 1—Objective: To familiarize your dog with both metal and leather articles.

First day

Start by giving your dog some experience in handling an article and associating it with your scent. With hands that are free of the odor of lotions, tobacco, and other adulterants, including the scent of another person, "rub up" an article, either metal or leather. Surveys indicate that dogs do not show a universal prejudice against handling metal, so take your choice. There is no point in debating how much rubbing is enough, so just rub up all of the bars and call it good. Next, and this is important, **hold the article close to your dog's nose so that he's prompted to smell it in close association with your hand.** This is a consistently used preliminary that will later be developed into a pattern to cue the dog when he sniffs your empty hand in the ring. Next, have your dog hold the object. Praise him for the act. Repeat the pattern a few times.

After this brief introduction, send the dog in a business-

The use of properly designed scent discrimination articles, such as these, will bring more satisfactory training results. The text explains why.

like way to make a few on-leash retrieves. "Businesslike" because that's the way it will be in the ring. Nurse him on kitchy-coo now and you'll have to wean him later. Praise him sincerely for a good performance. Continue this first session with a few short retrieves of the article from tall grass or leaves. This will give him practice in finding, or at least identifying, the article by scent. Don't deliberately cover it: just let it drop. Remember exactly where the article is, so if he quits hunting, you can correct him to it.

Finish the session when the dog is at a high point—not when he's contentious.

After a break that can include some other exercises, use the same familiarization program with the other kind of article.

Never will two articles bearing your scent be placed together in a discrimination exercise, so it would be harmful to place two together in training. Don't even work on them alternately at this point. Do the complete familiarizing process with one article, then, after a break, with the other. By the end of the first day, whether you work a single session or more on each article, your dog should be familiar with the sight and feel of the two kinds of articles that bear your scent.

Level 2—Objective: To give the dog experience in retrieving articles that are placed.

Second through eighth days

Begin the session by repeating some of the retrieve patterns previously used. Include some where grass or other cover prompts your dog to use his nose. When he is working without the slightest contention, put him on a **Sit-Stay** so he can watch you place an article a leash length away from him. Help him learn to depend on his scenting powers by placing the articles upwind, never downwind, from where he will start seeking so it's almost easier to smell an article than to see it. Return and send him. Repeat the pattern a half dozen times. This practice in retrieving something placed, not thrown, is a step toward meeting the demands of competition that will later be made.

Weight of the articles is no factor in training. This Chihuahua is carrying a Saint Bernard's article.

Retrieves from tall grass or leaves will give your dog practice in identifying an article by scent.

Probably your dog will retrieve as usual and win your praise. However, if he's so oriented to thrown objects that he doesn't go on your command, don't give him another word or gesture. He'll be "unconfused" faster and concentrate better if you correct him effectively to the article. Repeat the pattern until the dog is winning your praise every time you send him. Give him a bit of time to himself; then duplicate the patterns, using the other kind of article. Each day for a week, give your dog ten opportunities to smell and retrieve both kinds of articles bearing your scent. Some of these times place the article in fairly tall grass so that it becomes progressively more natural for him to use his nose as well as his eyes.

The more he depends on his nose in finding an article, the easier it will be for him to learn to discriminate between another person's scent and your own. Regardless of how long it takes, be positive that your dog has that foundation before you attempt the next level.

Level 3—Objective: To discriminate between the scents of two otherwise identical articles.

Ninth through twenty-eighth days

You've given your dog a lot of experience in retrieving an object that has always borne your scent. It is reasonable to believe that he can detect the difference between an article that bears your scent and an article that is identical except that it bears another's scent. "Or," you might be saying, "between one scent and many others." Correct, but for reasons of convenience and clarity in handling, we'll start with one **right** and one **wrong.**

Be certain that your scent does not get on the wrong article. If you believe that you might have contaminated all your articles with your scent by handling them, you will have to neutralize them before you start work. This can be done to metal articles by dipping them in soapy water and then rinsing them thoroughly in plain hot water, being careful not to handle them with your hands. A pair of salad tongs is useful for this

50

Use tongs if you place the "wrong" article yourself.

Can you tell which of these articles is tied down?

51

purpose. There is much that is not known about scent, even by those who claim to know all about it, so it's infinitely fairer to your dog to be meticulously careful in the handling of your articles. Think, so you won't be guilty of confusing your dog with contaminated articles.

Arrange for a helper to place articles for you if possible. Otherwise, you can place both articles yourself by using salad tongs to place a **wrong** article that someone pre-scented for you. You will find the tongs equally useful when a helper places the **right** article.

It's advisable to place the articles in the same set-up where your dog got his early experience in retrieving them. True, his actions might be more automatic than exploratory, and he might rush in and grab the first article that comes into his focus, but at least he's heading in the right direction in a familiar environment that will not distract from the essence of the pattern, which is to discriminate.

A device sometimes used in this earliest stage of **Scent Discrimination** is to make the **wrong** article more obviously wrong by anchoring it so that it would resist a dog's effort to lift it, thereby making the easily lifted **right** article more obviously right. There are many examples of set-ups made by fastening **wrong** articles onto plywood, masonite and pegboard, leaving only the **right** one subject to a dog's lift. Some of the cords and straps used as tie-downs are so wide and conspicuous that even a dog with faulty vision could see the difference from ten feet away.

If you choose to fasten the wrong articles, the author recommends anchors that make **wrong** and **right** articles alike in appearance. Both articles on page 51 have pieces of fine wire around their shafts. **What you don't see is that the wire on the wrong article is fastened to a spike that was driven into the ground.** It can be fastened to another surface if most trials in your area are held indoors.

Although the practice of tying down **wrong** articles is sometimes useful, it can introduce a problem. A good percentage of dogs will discover that the loose article is always the **right** one, and will test each article for movability, rather than for scent. So, even if you feel it might be helpful, don't depend on tie-downs for long. You might train a dog that discriminates by "feel." Remember—they'll all feel the same in the ring.

Have your helper rub up an article that is completely free of your scent, and place it, staked down if you prefer, a leash length from where you stand with your dog. Rub up a **right** article, of the same kind your helper takes from you with his tongs and places about a foot to one side of the **wrong** one. Later you and your dog will have your backs to such proceedings, but, until he discriminates, it would be well to work on pure discrimination without the complication of a turn.

When the set-up has been made, your helper should step back and order you to **Send your dog.** Send him exactly as you did when you placed an article yourself. Be sure you know the number as well as the location of the **right** article in case it gets moved during the action.

Even if you feel it was pure luck that took him to the **right** article without so much as a side glance at the other, praise him the instant he picks it up, and again when he retrieves it. What is sometimes labeled luck can be an ability we cannot fully understand. Luck or ability, if he gets the right article, you owe him praise.

Should you be blessed with a dog who sniffs each article in turn and then selects the **right** one, let your praise convince him that he's the greatest creature on earth. Be equally prompt in your praise if the **wrong** article was anchored and he tries to lift it, and, unsuccessful, turns to the **right** one and retrieves it.

Rejoice. He kept working and got the **right** one, which could have reminded him that success is easy with an article that bears your scent.

Questions often asked by trainers with problems concern dogs that:

1. Go to the **wrong** article and, when unable to lift it, quit working even though the **right** one is only a foot away.
2. Check both articles, then plead great confusion.
3. Refuse to go to the articles.

In any of the above cases, the handler would be justified in correcting the dog from the point of the refusal on to the

Giving your dog your scent serves as a cue telling him he will be sent to retrieve.

right article. This strong action would be fairer to the dog than giving him cues intended to remind him of what he already knows he should do. Such a correction can pose no great difficulty for the handler of an adequately motivated retriever. If you have the other kind, and find that the demands of selecting and retrieving a specific placed article are vastly different than the fun and games of a thrown, kitchy-coo dumbbell, you might feel that you have little going for you except your noble determination to tippy-toe across the bogs of reality and on to a U.D. even if it takes forty trials, five years, and a thousand dollars worth of entry fees and transportation.

Do not make the mistake of trying to correct a fun-and-games dog that has no realistic foundation in the same way that you would correct a solidly grounded dog who had been taught positive retrieving through reasonable, measured progressions. Instead, review pages 15 and 16 very carefully. It might help you come to a decision.

An anchor makes it almost impossible for a dog to retrieve the **wrong** article, but occasionally a dog will freeze onto it and try. With calm, deliberate handling the trainer should move in and flip it from his mouth by snagging a protruding end with a loop of his leash, and he should then be corrected to the **right** article.

Following the correction, the set-up should be repeated in a hurry and as many times as is necessary for the dog to succeed. Give your dog praise and something more each time he retrieves the **right** article. Tell him with your praise and a definite break that he's just completed a good job. It will help him to comprehend and remember the form of what he just did.

After the break, ask him to do the job again. A trainer working at the Utility level should be able to judge the number of consecutive experiences his dog needs at various levels for optimum learning.

Generally a good time to end a session at this level is when a dog has made two consecutive finds and retrieves, whether they were by chance or choice. Two such sessions on this first day of discriminating between two articles of the same material would be about right for the average dog. If you should hit some resistance, don't quit before you've accomplished such a reasonable objective or your dog will know you're a quitter.

Occasionally an excellent trainer will have difficulty in "breaking through" on the problem of discriminating by scent, even though his dog has been a fast learner in other respects, and the basic steps have been carefully and patiently taken. The dog seems almost unable to comprehend that there is a **right** smell and a **wrong** smell. There is a device that can make most dogs understand that one of the articles is more than merely **wrong**—that it is absolutely **taboo.** The **wrong** article is made taboo by applying the same principle used to make any distraction or temptation taboo. Make the **wrong** smell so redundantly tempting that the dog senses it is a deliberate plant, in the way that he recognizes other staged distractions as plants.

Simply have your helper rub up his **wrong** article with hands that are a bit fouled with bacon grease or another inviting odor, or, if you must work alone, by carefully dumping a pre-fouled article in place from an airtight jar. When your dog picks up the tempting article, snag it from his mouth in association with a loud **out,** and really correct him to the **right** article. This should be done with as much finality as you would use to correct him if he broke a **Sit-Stay** to visit a planted cat. Properly done, this will cause him to reject any article that bears a scent other than yours as a taboo. Gradually, all **wrong** articles, whether temptingly scented or not, take on this taboo status.

Experienced trainers who read this book might question whether the closeness of the taboo scent to the **right** article, plus the vagaries of air currents, might not make a dog "pile-shy" with the result that he would avoid going to the set-up or would circle it warily. Because of such a possibility, I checked its effect on the wide variety of dogs in my Utility classes.

Understand that all of these dogs, from Toys to St. Bernards, were positive retrievers and all had a background of success in finding an article that bore the handler's scent before they were asked to discriminate. Because of such a good foundation, the few that showed a temporary pile-shyness could be made to go to the set-up and concentrate on finding the **right** one. If these dogs had been motivated solely by play, the results might have been less favorable. In a great many cases the use of this **taboo leverage** was the catalyst that enabled a dog with a block to comprehend and break through on discrimination.

Caution. Think. It would be disastrous to contaminate your **right** article with the taboo scent. Keep the scented article in an airtight jar for future use, and keep the jar away from your other articles. The above procedures, including the taboo scent if you feel you need it, should bring even the slower dog to a point where he discriminates reliably between one **right** and one **wrong** article.

In a Utility class some dogs discriminate almost from the very start and will work reliably after a week of experience. Others seem to waver between comprehension and confusion; and require from two to three weeks of top handling and patience to become solid. A few, because of their own deficiencies, less capable handlers or insufficient work, will appear to be oblivious to any difference in scents, but finally, after six or seven weeks of grinding, see the light.

Don't let what appears to be a stone wall dishearten you. Work thoughtfully, consistently and with determination. You'll win out.

Level 4—Objective: Equal competence with the second kind of articles.

Twenty-ninth through thirty-fifth days

When your dog discriminates reliably between scents on articles of the same kind, work to bring him to the same competence with two of the other kind. Your helper should alternate the positions of the **right** and **wrong** articles as soon as your dog is working smoothly. This will prevent him from discriminating by location. It's best not to make the switch while you're working out a problem.

Do not mix the two kinds of articles until you are told to do so.

Level 5—Objective: To discriminate among three articles, and to add the **turn and send** to the pattern.

Thirty-sixth through forty-fifth days

Each article that is added to the set-ups brings with it some slight problems for the handler and dog. The handler must be even more careful to remember the number and position of the **right** article, particularly if it should be struck by the dog's foot or nose during the scuffle of a correction. When more than two articles are used, the dog will no longer have an even chance of finding the **right** one by pure luck. True, luck can take him to the **right** one, but the odds will now require that he must more often sniff and reject the **wrong** ones before succeeding.

Your helper should place two **wrong** articles, of the same kind and anchored if you wish, while you and your dog watch from a leash length away. You will be permitted to watch the **wrong** articles being placed in the ring, so this part of the pattern is something that can develop into a legitimate cue to your dog. With his tongs, your helper should take the **right** article from you and place it about a foot from the others. The position of the articles in relation to each other is not important as long as it is varied occasionally, and leaves room for clean corrections.

Don't worry that your dog might mark the last article put down as the **right** one. Soon his back will be turned as the **right** one is placed.

As always, you'll have to praise him even if luck should take him directly to the **right** one. If he smells a single **wrong** one and then lucks into the **right** one, rejoice and praise him. If he should sniff two **wrong** ones and then picks up the **right** one, you and your dog are both to be congratulated. Praise him and keep on praising him as you walk around on a short break that tells him he just did something great.

Should his "discrimination" consist of methodically trying to lift one or more anchored articles, without any visible sniff before he lucks into the **right** one, you'll still owe him some praise—about one half-word.

However, you've just seen evidence that further use of the tie-downs will do more harm than good.

Any continued effort to pull on a **wrong** article should give you time and reason to jump in and snag it from his mouth and then correct him to the **right** one.

Repeat work on the above set-ups until your dog has discriminated and retrieved two consecutive times; then end the session.

In addition to discriminating by trying to lift the articles, a sharp dog can discriminate by voice. Yup, by voice. As he touches each article in turn, he will listen for a word of encouragement to tell him he has zeroed in on the **right** one. This poses a problem. Every trainer realizes the importance of praising for the essence of the moment, which in this case means when discrimination is taking place. Most dogs eventually come to depend on the scent that has always been associated with the word of approval, but some do not. It is a fact of life that the trainer must cut the "vocal umbilical cord" to such a dog, let him make a mistake, even if the mistake is only waiting, and then correct him to the **right** article.

Any apprehension that this "cold-turkey" maneuver might inhibit your dog means that you lack confidence in your ability to make him retrieve.

Repeat work on the above set-ups until your dog has correctly discriminated two consecutive times, then end the session. Give him another such session during the day.

Your dog will gain in ability and confidence if for the next ten days you will give him the same kind and amount of experiences described for the first day of this level. This would be a reasonable period for the average dog, but be honest in your judgment and continue the daily program until he discriminates smoothly and reliably, regardless of how many days are required. It would be much more difficult to resolve basic problems at a later level where more articles are added to your set-ups and both kinds are combined.

Add a foot each day to the distance you send your dog until he is going about fifteen feet from where he is sent to where the articles are placed. When you've extended the re-

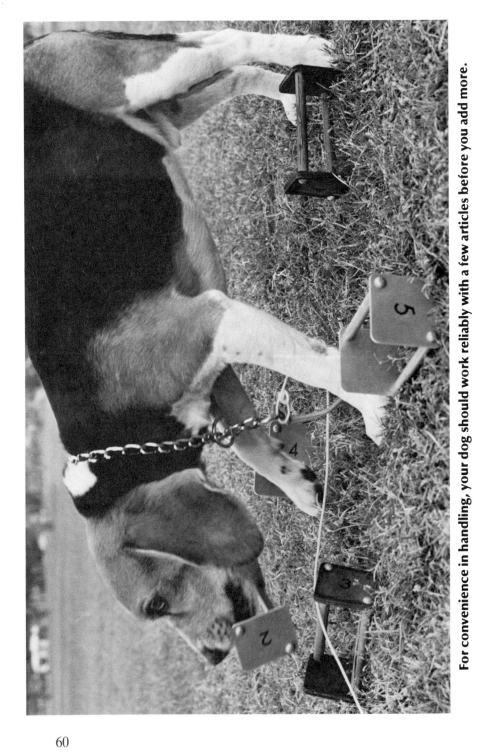

For convenience in handling, your dog should work reliably with a few articles before you add more.

trieve to that distance, you will be ready to turn and send your dog in the regulation manner.

You and your dog will always be permitted to watch the judge or steward place all of the **wrong** articles; then you will stand with your back to the set-up while you rub up an article and place it on the judge's work sheet, and while the judge places it among the **wrong** ones. When the judge says **Send your dog** you may give your scent to the dog by gently touching his nose, and give him a command to **Heel** as you turn to face the articles with the dog in the **Heel position.** You may then tell him to fetch.

This handling pattern gives you time to align and focus the dog with a **Sit,** and is much more logical than the old way of turning and sending the dog in one fluid motion which did little to focus him and often sent him on a wrong tangent.

Level 6—Objective: Discrimination among both kinds of articles.

Forth-sixth through sixty-fourth days

Until now your dog has selected a **right** article from others of the same material and identical in appearance. This was so that the sole difference was in scent and so that your dog would not be led to believe that any article of a different appearance than the one with your scent must be wrong. Now he must begin the exercise of finding the one article that bears your scent from among **wrong** ones of both kinds that are placed nearby.

Have your helper rub up and place four articles, two leather and two metal, in a set-up. Rub up an article, either metal or leather, which your helper should take with his tongs and place among the four **wrong** ones.

By now your dog has learned that discrimination can only be made by scent, so the number and kinds of articles will not be an acceptable reason for confusion, but we have limited the number of articles in the set-ups so that needed corrections

Use a variety of distractions to test your dog's reliability.

could be made more cleanly. Obviously, as we add more articles any goldbricking or goofing must be corrected as it was in the earlier stages even though handling will be a bit more difficult.

When your dog has been praised for a good performance, repeat the entire pattern, using the other kind of **right** article, and changing the relative positions of the **one right** one with the **four wrong** ones. At the moment he brings you this second kind of **right** article, tell him with your praise and attitude that he has finished a job. Give him a break. To keep dinging away after he has completed the exercise will prevent him from feeling the accomplishment which is part of the picture you want him to have.

Two or three of the above exercises, separated by breaks, should be sufficient for the first day.

Work just as you did on the first day. Hold to the pattern of using two kinds of **right** articles, one at a time, among the four **wrong** ones for twenty days. By the end of that time, your dog should be doing the exercise smoothly.

Level 7—Objective: To make the dog solid in working around distractions.

Sixty-fifth through seventy-first days

The handler whose dog is motivated solely by his desire to please sometimes becomes uneasy when it occurs to him that the dog might have to work in a ring exposed to temptations. These could distract such a dog from working to please his master.

The realistic trainer makes tempting sights, sounds and smells a part of his training environment. In this way the dog learns that he must work around distractions whether or not it pleases him to do so.

There is a lot of leverage in using legitimate temptations in combination with corrections to bring a dog to the point where distractions serve to herd his mind back to the job at hand.

Give your dog a solid week or more of this realistic experience, if it is needed, to bring him to the point where distractions seem only to remind him of what you will expect.

Level 8—Objective: The complete **Scent Discrimination** exercise.

Until training is completed

Now that your dog seldom needs a correction, you can conveniently add another of each kind of article. Work with the six **wrong** ones for as long as you feel is advisable, then add the final two articles so that your dog will have to discriminate between all the articles in a regulation set-up: eight **wrong** ones and, in turn, each of your **right** ones.

Guard against any tendency to always rub up the same **right** ones. Be realistic. Practice with clean articles. Let your helper tell you which numbers to rub up and use as **right** ones. Now that you are working with the regulation number of articles, it would be a convenience to have an extra one of each material so that you will have a spare in case a **right** one gets fouled.

When it seems that you have worked out all your problems on the exercise, begin to practice it as part of the program explained in Chapter 7.

AKC REGULATIONS FOR
THE SCENT DISCRIMINATION EXERCISE

Section 7. **Scent Discrimination.** The principal features of these exercises are the selection of the handler's article from among the other articles by scent alone, and the prompt delivery of the right article to the handler.

The Judge will ask, "Are you Ready?" immediately prior to taking the article from the handler. The taking of the article from the handler will be considered to be the first order and scoring of the exercise will begin at that time. The remaining orders are "Send your dog," "Take it," and "Finish."

In each of these two exercises the dog must select by scent alone and retrieve an article which has been handled by its handler. The articles shall be provided by the handler and shall consist of two sets, each comprised of five identical objects not more than six inches in length, which may be items of everyday use. One set shall be made entirely of rigid metal, and one of leather of such design that nothing but leather is visible except for the minimum amount of thread or metal necessary to hold the object together. The articles in each set must be legibly numbered, each with a different number, and must be approved by the Judge.

The handler shall present all 10 articles to the Judge, who shall designate one from each set and make written note of the numbers of the two articles he has selected. These two handler's articles shall be placed on a table or chair within the ring until picked up by the handler, who shall hold in his hand only one article at a time. The Judge or Steward will handle each of the remaining 8 articles as he places them on the floor or ground at random and about six inches apart, with the closest article being about 20 feet from the handler and the dog. Before the dog is sent, the Judge must make sure that the articles are visible to the dog and handler, and that the articles are properly separated so that there will be no confusion of scent between the articles.

Handler and dog shall turn around after watching the Judge or Steward spread the articles, and shall remain facing away from those articles until the Judge has taken the handler's scented article and given the order, "Send your dog."

The handler may use either article first, but must relinquish each one immediately when ordered by the Judge. The Judge shall make certain that the handler imparts his scent to each article only with his hands and that, between the time the handler picks up each article and the time he gives it to the Judge, the article is held continuously in the handler's hands, which must remain in plain sight.

On order from the Judge, the handler will immediately place his article on the Judge's book or work sheet. The Judge, without touching the article with his hands, will place it among those on the ground or floor.

On order from the Judge to "Send your dog," the handler may give the command to heel and will turn in place, right or left, to face the articles. The handler will come to a halt with the dog sitting in the heel position. The handler shall then give the command or signal to retrieve. The handler may give his scent to the dog by gently touching the dog's nose with the palm of one open hand, but this may only be done while the dog and handler have their backs to the articles and the arm and hand must be returned to a natural position before handler and dog turn to face the articles.

The dog shall go at a brisk trot or gallop directly to the articles. It may take any reasonable time to select the right article, but only provided it works continuously. After picking up the right article the dog shall return at a brisk trot or gallop and complete the exercise as in the Retrieve on the Flat.

These procedures shall be followed for both articles. Should a dog retrieve a wrong article in the first exercise, that article shall be placed on the table or chair. The correct article must be removed, and the second exercise shall be conducted with one less article on the ground or floor.

Section 8. **Scent Discrimination, Scoring.** Deductions shall be the same as in the Novice Recall and the Retrieve on the Flat. In addition, a dog that fails to go out to the group of articles, or retrieves a wrong article, or fails to bring the right article to the handler, must be scored zero for the particular exercise.

Substantial deductions shall be made for a dog that picks up a wrong article, even though he puts it down again immediately, for any roughness by the handler in imparting his scent to the dog, and for the handler not turning in place.

Minor or substantial deductions, depending on the circumstances in each case, shall be made for a dog that is slow or inattentive, that does not go directly to the articles, or that does not work continuously, or for any excessive motions by the handler in turning to face the articles. There shall be no penalty for a dog that takes a reasonably long time examining the articles provided the dog works smartly and continuously.

4

The Directed Retrieve

$\mathbf{Y}$OU MIGHT ASK, at first consideration, how and why any dog could fail such a simple exercise as the **Directed Retrieve.** How? The dog goes for the wrong glove. Why? His trainer probably tried to make him dependent on direction by always directing him toward a glove that the dog could see. Such a sight-oriented dog will often concentrate on the first glove he sees, regardless of the direction the handler gives him. This is particularly true when the exercise is taught as a game. Watch the dogs perform in the Utility ring. You will often see a dog eager to head for the first glove that caught his eye, oblivious to the pointing and prayers of his handler. You will find it worthwhile to make your dog dependent on you for the direction in which he should go, even though white gloves are falling like blossoms to the right and left of him.

The following program, based on Blind Retrieving, will make any solid retriever more dependent on where he's sent than on what he first sees.

Dig holes that are barely big enough to conceal a glove from your dog.

Level 1—Objective: To Blind Retrieve number one glove.

First through sixth days

Because success in giving your direction will depend somewhat on smooth coordination between you and your dog, we'll work in a pattern very similar to the angles of the retrieves in an average ring. The numbers one and three gloves would be spaced at about thirty-degree angles to the direction a handler faces as he looks down the centerline at the number two glove. Number one would be to the handler's left and number three to his right. It would be about twenty-two feet from the handler's position between the jumps down the centerline to the number two glove, and about thirty feet to each of the other gloves. Even though you'll be working at a short distance for a while, it's important that the angles to the side gloves be close to average so that, later, the turns you practice will feel natural in the ring. Mark what would be the approximate lines to the gloves by tying strips of rag on the ring rope so you will have prominent focal points.

Next, on each of the lines that would run from the sending point between the jumps toward your markers, measure out from the sending point six or eight feet toward each marker and dig a small hole that could barely conceal a glove. A hole about five inches in diameter and six inches deep would conceal a glove from most dogs if they were seated six to eight feet away. It makes no difference whether your dog can see a hole as long as he can not see a glove in it. **Important:** check the holes from what will be your dog's location and level to be sure they will conceal a glove.

Before we start on the **Blind Retrieving,** have your dog hold a glove a few times, and then toss it out several times so he can handle it on a few short retrieves. Now that he's familiar with the glove, on to the blind retrieving.

Before you bring your dog to the area, crumple the glove and shove it firmly down into the number one hole, which would be the one to your left if you were facing down the centerline. Heel your dog to the sending spot, the check-cord attached to his collar. He must sit squarely facing the number one hole.

Look to see that the check-cord will not foul on your feet or his as you stand close beside him. If necessary, bend your legs and body so you can extend your left arm and hand, rigidly and horizontally, along the right side of your dog's head and at his eye level in your best effort to do two things: (1) Indicate the direction you want him to go. (2) Block from his vision anything to the right of the direction you are pointing. Don't let your hand or arm touch the dog. Hold your arm motionless until the dog seems to be looking in the right direction, then give your **fetch** command. A solid retriever is almost certain to move out on command; and only a few steps forward will enable him to see the white glove in the hole.

Praise him enthusiastically if he makes the retrieve.

What if a dog doesn't move out or fails to follow through on the retrieve?

Correct him all the way to the glove. Convince him that he must make the retrieve just as he did when you tossed the glove out for him. No, we won't give him the second command. We won't dance out on tippy-toes and try to encourage him to have funny-wunny with the nice glove. Such things would not clarify as much as they would confuse. It's better that he learn cold turkey that **he must go out on one command to retrieve a familiar object that will be in the direction you indicate.** Give him the necessity, and praise for the accomplishment. He'll do the learning. He'll get just as much fun out of the hidey-seekey if he knows he must seek as he would if you called it a game. In fact, more.

Set up the problem as before. This time, if he's any kind of a retriever, he'll move out on your command. Again, lots of praise.

Even though it looks "too easy," continue to work in this same short pattern. **It will give your dog confidence in your ability to direct him to what he cannot see at the moment he is sent.** When he has made five successive willing retrieves, end your work on the exercise for this period.

Give your dog a break, or work on something dissimilar, such as the **Signal exercise,** then work again on the number one hole until he has made five more consecutive retrieves.

A good signal.

After this much success it would be well to end work on the exercise for the day.

Two more days of the experience described above should convince your dog that there will always be a glove in the direction you indicate. When he has that foundation, the two of you will be prepared to work on the coordinated turn and direction needed to send him to the number one glove in the regulation manner.

When doing the **Directed Retrieve** in the ring, you will be required to stand with your dog in the **Heel position** at a point midway between the jumps and with your back to the end where the steward will place the gloves. It is from this position that the two of you will turn to face toward the indicated glove. You and your dog will both need practice in turning accurately and smoothly so that the turn will face him squarely to the glove as you prepare to direct him. First, practice without your dog until you are turning smoothly, then work at coordinating the action with your dog in sessions that are separate from the retrieving lessons.

In a relaxed manner, turn in place to the right on your right heel until you face the marker you placed to give direction to the number one position.

Bring your left foot around to a comfortable position in relation to your right so that it will seem solid and natural for you to descend and align your left arm to give direction. When it feels easy and stable for you to make the turn, practice with your dog. Just the basic steps: no bend or direction which, without the actual retrieve, would cause him to doubt and ignore your signals. Give a **Heel** command as you turn; and, if needed, use your leash to get prompt and accurate compliance. Your left side will actually move a couple of feet from the radius of your turn which will make the need to **Heel** plain to your dog. Obviously, he must sit straight in order for you to direct him to the hole.

When you and your dog are a smoothly turning team, combine the turn with your complete direction. You will both gain in confidence and ability by working on the number one glove just as you did, and for as long as you did on the straightway, except now you will turn and direct him.

72

**A good retriever will start on command—and in the right direc-
tion.**

Level 2—Objective: Turn and retrieve from number two hole.

Seventh through twelfth days

Follow the same principles and time increments as you work on the number two hole as you did when you worked on the previous pattern. Do not place a glove in other than the number two hole. Do not be tempted to alternate between positions. Use the full three days to give your dog practice in going straight from the sending spot to blind retrieve just as though he had never been worked on the first position.

If memory causes him to ignore your direction and go to the number one hole, let him find the hole empty, then correct him all the way to the glove.

Without your dog, practice your own footwork in turning to face the new position, so that after the dog has finished his three days of straightway retrieving, you will be prepared to practice the new turn with him.

The right turn to face position number two is actually a right about-turn of a full 180 degrees. Pivot on your right heel and left toe, then bring the left foot up into good position beside your right. When you are making the turn smoothly and are ending up with the balance needed to give direction, introduce your dog to the turn.

Remember you are turning in place, but your dog must make a half circle around you, so don't accuse him of slowness. Don't start the turn before you give the **Heel** command. Until your turns consistently face the dog squarely to the hole, do not try to give him any arm direction.

Work until you feel that it is easy to turn and line both your dog and your arm up in the right direction, then start practice in actually turning and sending the dog. Give him as much practice on the turn and retrieve as you did on sending him straightway.

Level 3—Objective: Turn and retrieve from number three hole.

Thirteenth through eighteenth days

You can gain much by giving your dog equal orientation to the way all these positions lie in relation to the ring geography and the ropes. Don't dismiss as "too easy, or boring" the task of working three days on carefully placing the glove in a hole and sending the dog straightway to it, before you turn and send him. Do not alternate between holes, nor have a glove in any but the number three position. Again, if memory sends him to a former location for a glove, let him see the hole is empty, but then correct him all the way to the glove. No! To let him check locations until he found the glove would not serve a purpose. The essence of the exercise is for him to take your direction, not find by hidey-seekey. He should only taste success when he goes straight to where you direct. Remember: **Directed Retrieve.**

Aside from the work on the straightway retrieves, work without your dog to develop the turn to the number three position.

There are good reasons why you should turn to the left to face the number three glove: (A) Your dog will learn that a left turn will always be part of the direction to only that glove. (B) A left turn faces the dog to the number three hole by the shortest and easiest route. Obviously, you will turn in place on the left heel and bring your right foot into position. Practice the left turn without the dog during his three days of work on the straight retrieves from the number three hole.

The turn to the left requires that a dog back up a bit to hold the **Heel** relationship. The dog that finishes by going directly to the left side and turning to face the same direction as the handler, will almost automatically adjust to the handler's turn and **Heel** command. If not, he can be taught to back up with the same leash action that tidied up the finish in Novice work. Should your dog be one that finished by circling around you, you can easily teach him to back up and readjust to your changed position when he hears your command.

For a while, instead of using that smooth left turn you've developed, where you pivot on the left heel, pivot on the right heel, awkward though it might seem, and then take a barricading step out to the left as you turn, which gives the dog a good physical reason to back up in order to be at your side as you face the glove. Use the word **left** or any other suitable word. **Back** is also a good word of command unless you use it for another purpose as many handlers do. He'll soon learn that your word means you'll turn left. When he's backing around accurately and reliably to stay out of your leg's way on the left turns, you can resume your turning in place on your left heel. If it's needed, crooked sits can be corrected with a combination of your left hand and sharp leash action.

The same principles and techniques will apply in handling your dog on the turn and send to the number three position as when you worked him on the first two holes. Give him his honest measure of work on the position before you attempt the next level.

Level 4—Objective: Retrieves in varied directions.

Nineteenth through twenty-fifth days

Now that you've polished your turns and direction to each of the holes as separate projects, you should be qualified to work on all three retrieves in any order you choose. But not in **close order.** Remember, the **Directed Retrieve is a one-glove exercise.** When your dog has made a good retrieve, praise him and make him feel the exercise is finished. **Don't follow that good retrieve by sending him for a second glove during the same session.**

Observe the following pattern closely. Start in any order you wish, but put a glove only in the hole to which you will send him. Then, if he goes against your direction and scrambles to the wrong hole, it will be empty and you can correct him to the right spot. It's simply more of "If he goes wrong, nothing. If he takes direction, the glove."

When he performs well, praise him in a way that tells him

he's done a complete exercise. Then **Heel** him around the area a couple of times or do some simple **Novice exercise** to take his thoughts from the glove.

Why?

Here's why: At the level of **Utility work,** many dogs have developed mentally to a point where they memorize patterns to a cursed degree. Your dog will only make one **Directed Retrieve** when working in the ring, and confusion can be generated by having him make two or more practice retrieves in close order. He might possibly look for a second glove when you send him out on the **Directed Jump exercise** which, since the last change in Obedience Regulations, immediately follows the **Directed Retrieve.** More will be said of this in a later chapter. After a mind-clearing break, which could be an unrelated kind of work, have him retrieve from another hole. This could be a moment of trial for your dog. He might try to head back for the hole you last worked, which should now be empty. Be prepared to correct. When he has made a retrieve without a problem, make him feel that the job is finished by your praise and a little work on another exercise. Then give him a break.

Repeat the pattern on the last hole. In any order, but with a break in between the retrieves, work until your dog has made two successful retrieves from each hole. It is well to vary the order of your direction so neither of you will develop a favorite angle. Remember the break after each retrieve.

Level 5—Objective: To extend the length of retrieves.

Twenty-sixth through thirty-first days

Dig a new hole on each of the lines about one half the distance from where your dog has been retrieving to where the gloves will eventually be placed in your mockup ring. This means you'll be sending him approximately eighteen feet to the holes on the angles and a bit shorter distance to the hole in the middle. Fill up the old holes.

Use the same general pattern of work that you did when working on the shorter retrieves. Your dog might stop and dawdle a bit where the old holes were located, but he'll soon learn to keep going until he reaches the glove. Work him on your check cord so he cannot avoid a needed correction. He can use the experience in going farther than he has been, so work him a couple of extra days at the new distances. The length and geography of your patterns should feel good to you before you attempt the next level.

Level 6—Objective: To Blind Retrieve at ring distances.

Thirty-second through thirty-seventh days

A perusal of *Obedience Regulations* would indicate that a Utility ring forty feet wide and fifty feet long would be an acceptable size upon which to base an average length of the retrieves. In such a ring your dog would travel from where he is sent in mid-ring approximately thirty feet to gloves **one** and **three** and about twenty-two feet to glove number **two.** Match these glove positions as closely as you can in your own ring. Dig a hole where each of the gloves would be. Cover the other holes.

Work at these actual ring distances just as you did when the holes were closer. Because you worked with the correct angles from the start, your turns and directing will be about the same. The new distances might bother your dog temporarily, but consistent work will iron out the problems. Continue to vary the order in which you work, and make him feel that each retrieve is a complete exercise.

Be sure that your dog works reliably and willingly before you face the changes you'll encounter at the next level.

Level 7—Objective: To take direction to an unseen glove with another glove in sight.

Thirty-eighth through the forty-seventh days

Stand with your dog just as you would while the gloves were being placed in a regulation ring. **Your helper should now**

At this level, a dog should take direction to an unseen glove with another glove in sight.

conceal a glove in the number one hole and drop another in plain sight beside the number three hole. Be ready to grab the check-cord and correct if needed. Turn and direct the dog to the glove in the hole. If at any point he veers from the line toward the visible glove, check him and hold him back while you go to him, then correct him to the glove in the hole.

"Ooh, ooh, ooh—unfair," you say, "with that other glove in plain sight!"

If you're an "Ooh-ooh," take a look at some facts: (A) Every time he followed the direction of your hand, your dog found a glove and was praised for his success. (B) The whole point of blind retrieving is to orient him to your direction instead of sight. (C) When the **wrong** glove is 70 degrees from the direction you gave him, surely a mistake is big enough for your dog to feel. Focus by sight is the very thing that causes a dog to head for the first glove he sees in the ring. Make no mistake, he knows what your direction means, so don't underestimate your dog's ability to understand the situation.

Consider the case of a dog in a retriever trial, who, on an optional retrieve, might be sent a hundred yards to intercept a wind-driven fall before it drifts away, instead of being permitted to go to an easy fall that he had just marked. "Ooh-ooh," indeed.

What you are asking is fair, so work and work at convincing your dog that he'd better go to the glove in the direction you point, rather than to angle off to the first one that catches his eye.

Vary the order of the **lines** you give him and the placement of the visible glove. In other respects, continue to follow your previous patterns of work: A successful retrieve then an interim exercise before you send him for another glove. After ten days of work, you should be able to send him to a glove in a hole with one visible at each of the other two positions.

Be honest in your appraisal of your dog and yourself before you go to the next level.

No matter which glove your dog sees first, he should go where he's sent.

Level 8—Objective: To work with three gloves in sight.

Forty-eighth through sixty-fourth days

You might think that, because you can turn and send a dog to a glove in a hole, there could be no problem in directing him to a glove in plain sight. Do not be overconfident. Be prepared.

Cover up the holes. Take your position with your dog, cord attached, while your helper drops a glove at each of the three positions. Unless you want to work on a particular glove to correct a weakness, your helper should indicate by number the glove to be retrieved.

Turn, direct and send your dog to the designated glove. There is a small chance that your dog could be confused by being directed to a visible glove, but remember, even when he started "blind," the glove in the hole could be seen at least several feet before he got to it. It became visible when he traveled straight ahead in the direction you sent him. So to retrieve a visible glove isn't actually a new task. Praise him and end the exercise in the usual way. That's it—only one glove each time you do the **Directed Retrieve.** If necessary, correct him and work until you can praise him for a good performance. Then end the exercise. After the break, send him for a different glove.

Because the **Directed Retrieve** now immediately precedes the **Directed Jump** in the Utility routine, and the dog is sent in the same direction for both exercises, there are advantages in practicing the first as a "one and done" exercise so the dog doesn't go looking for a second glove. Again, more on this in the practice section.

Level 9—Objective: To polish handling and performance.

Until training is completed

If your dog works reliably on all three gloves, you're probably doing a good job of directing him. Unreliability on one particular glove could mean you need to improve your handling in that direction. You might have developed a fault of which you are unaware. Have a knowledgeable person check your handling and the dog's response on the problem glove. He might see an error in action or timing. Almost as important, he might see a disqualifying fault such as moving from place on a turn or an improper signal that would bring a penalty in the ring.

Work your dog in a variety of environments so that no future ring conditions will seem unusual.

Even when you feel that you've ironed out all the problems and are ready to do your practicing as part of the ring routine, concentrate on being consistent in the actions and voice you use to send your dog on a **Directed Retrieve.**

AKC REGULATIONS FOR
THE DIRECTED RETRIEVE

Section 9. **Directed Retrieve.** The principal features of the exercise are that the dog stay until directed to retrieve, that it go directly to the designated glove, and that it retrieve promptly. The orders for the exercise are "One," "Two" or "Three," "Take it" and "Finish." In this exercise the handler will provide three predominantly white, cotton work gloves, which must be open and must be approved by the Judge. The handler will stand with his back to the unobstructed end of the ring with his dog sitting in the Heel position midway between and in line with the two jumps. The Judge or Steward will then drop the three gloves across the end of the ring, while the handler and dog are facing the opposite direction, one glove in each corner and one in the center, about 3 feet from the end of the ring and for the corner gloves, about 3 feet from the side of the ring. All three gloves will be clearly visible to the dog and handler, when the handler turns to face the glove designated by the Judge. There shall be no table or chair at this end of the ring.

The gloves shall be designated "One," "Two" or "Three" reading from left to right when the handler turns and faces the gloves. The Judge will give the order "One," or "Two" or "Three." The handler then may give the command to Heel and turn in place, right or left to face the designated glove. The handler will come to a halt with the dog sitting in the Heel position. The handler shall not touch the dog to get it into position nor may he reposition the dog. The handler will then give his dog the direction to the designated glove with a single motion of his left hand and arm along the right side of the dog, and will give a verbal command to retrieve either simultaneously with or immediately following the giving of the direction. The dog shall then go directly to the glove at a brisk trot or gallop and retrieve it without unnecessary mouthing or playing with it, completing the exercise as in the Retrieve on the Flat.

The handler may bend his body and knees to the extent necessary in giving the direction to the dog, after which the handler will stand erect in a natural position with his arms at his sides.

The exercise shall consist of a single retrieve. Prior to the start of judging the Judge shall make the decision to either assign the gloves to dogs so that successive dogs in catalog order will have different gloves, or to assign the gloves as the dogs appear in the ring for judging so that two successive dogs do not receive the same glove. In either case each glove shall be used approximately the same number of times.

Section 10. **Directed Retrieve, Scoring.** All applicable penalties listed under the Novice Recall and the Retrieve on the Flat shall apply. In addition, a score of zero is required for any commands or signals by the handler, after turning, to position the dog to face the designated glove, for not going directly to the designated glove, or for not retrieving the glove.

Depending on the extent, a substantial deduction even to the point of zero shall be made for not turning in place or not turning to face the designated glove.

Depending on the extent, a minor to substantial deduction shall be made for a handler who touches the dog or uses excessive motions while turning to face the glove.

Depending on the extent, substantial or minor deductions shall be made for a handler who over-turns, or touches the dog or uses excessive motions while turning to face the glove.

After your dog has been introduced to the dowel as the text describes, have him retrieve it from the top of the cover at a leash length.

5

The Moving Stand and Examination

THE AMERICAN KENNEL CLUB amended the Utility Regulations as of March 1, 1989, and one of the effects was to replace the Group Examination with the Moving Stand and Examination. The change has made it unnecessary for a dog to hold a stand for the long period required by the Group Examination, but be aware of the two demands that are now regarded more critically. Your dog's attitude toward the judge and any moves he might make when on the Stand will be more apparent than they would be in the Group exercise. So, during the time you are working on the Moving Stand component, practice placing the dog for the Stand for Examination exercise just as you did in Novice work to make him solid under pressure.

Level 1—Objective: The dog should **Stand** and hold that position when the handler commands and/or signals him to do so while walking at **Heel** and faces him from one step in front, and return to the **Heel** position when commanded and/or signalled to do so. He should be very stable when approached and examined by a "judge" in practice separate from the Stand component.

Begin with your dog sitting at your side in the **Heel** position. Give him a **Heel** command or signal as you start walking in a normal way. Take four or five steps and give a **Stand** command and/or a signal without turning toward him. Use the same signal you give him when you leave him on the **Stand** in the Signal Exercise, but don't stop and face him until you've gone a step in front of him.

If he coasts forward or moves after the command, correct him. Thrust him back to position with a right-hand grip on the collar that won't allow it to constrict, which might cue him to sit. Avoid turning him around to get him back into position. Thrust him straight back to where he was commanded to stand, using your right hand on his collar, with your left hand free to pop him under the loin if he tries to sit.

When he is standing firmly, face him from no farther than one step out in front so he won't confuse coming toward you with a recall, which would require him to sit in front of you when you command and/or signal him to the **Heel** position. Work for good finishes just as you did on the Novice and Open levels. When you've successfully completed the above pattern, praise him and give him a short break before you repeat the pattern.

Work him on seven or eight of these patterns during at least ten daily sessions, more if needed, to reach a point where he stops on the **Stand** promptly, stays solidly in position and finishes without any confusion before you extend the pattern.

So that you are prepared to correct any disobedience or inaccuracies, work him only on leash until you are told to do differently.

Level 2—Objective: By the end of the level the dog should work in patterns that are equal to what will be required in the ring, but he should still be equipped with a light line so any needed corrections can be made smoothly.

Start with the dog at **Heel** on leash as usual, and after going the usual four or five steps command and/or signal, but instead of taking one step beyond where the dog stands, take two steps and turn to face him. After he holds the position for a few seconds, command and/or signal for him to return to the **Heel** position. Praise him and give him his break and work him on an exercise that's so simple you know he'll perform it without contention.

This technique of backwashing the feeling of success and confidence from a familiar exercise that a dog does well onto an exercise he is learning is a reinforcement that you will find useful and very interesting.

There is a good reason to use both a command and/or a signal to tell the dog to do the **Moving Stand,** and when you have him move from the **Stand** directly to the **Heel** position. The possibility of a dog missing the cue to stand is much less when he gets both the verbal and visual directions. And when you use both to bring him from the **Stand** to the **Heel** position, you will help him avoid any confusion with the **Recall,** which requires him to sit in front of you before finishing.

Practice the usual number of times on the exercise as described above for as many daily periods as are needed until your dog is performing the complete pattern reliably and accurately without the need of any corrections.

Level 3—Objective: To polish for the Ring.

From now on practice with the demands of the Utility Ring in mind. Mock up a ring of the same size and similarly equipped as the one described in the *Obedience Regulations.*

Take the same number of steps with the dog at **Heel** before you **Stand** him. Practice walking the way you will walk when handling in the ring. Gradually increase the distance from where he stands to where you face him, so he'll get practice in going directly to the **Heel** position from the maximum distance of about ten or twelve feet.

Be certain the person who serves as a "judge" is familiar with the Regulations so you will be practicing in a way that makes you an acceptable handler in the ring. Your judge should give you your instructions properly. Have him "examine" your dog a bit more thoroughly than would be the case in a show.

Practice combining your command and signal in a way that is acceptable and still gives the maximum emphasis.

STABILIZING A NERVOUS OR FIDGETY DOG

Occasionally there is a dog who learns the mechanics of an exercise very easily but seems to lack stability when he is in a strange environment. If you have a dog that is shy because of heredity, or has been made that way through undeserved reassurance, you should resort to that motivation called "necessity." He can be made stable by the use of lots of **Sit-Stays,** on leash, with strange occurrences positioned unusually close to him. When he has been told to **Stay,** he should stay. If he breaks, correct him in such a way that he's propelled back to position. You might be surprised to see how quickly he'll become concerned with what will inevitably happen to him if he moves, rather than with what a bogeyman might do to him if he holds the position. Obviously, when he holds the position until you move him, he'll get his praise for his bravery.

In many obedience clinics the author has demonstrated how rapidly an insecure dog can be made to concentrate on not moving when approached by a "judge" who wore glasses, walked with a limp or threatened in some other way.

TO CORRECT SHIFTING

Sometimes a dog that is very bold and obedient will do a good job of holding a location but will unconsciously move one or more of his feet around a bit. The fact that in his own mind he is obediently holding his position demands that any corrections be made with the utmost clarity. You must make your dog conscious of such movements before you can correct him. Use a "Donut." It will make the surface around the dog's foot feel different from the surface where his foot is. Cut two semicircles out of thin plywood of such dimensions that they can be placed together to encircle your dog's foot with about a half-inch clearance all around his pad. The outside diameter of the "donut" should fit comfortably between the dog's feet. When he moves a foot and puts it down onto a strange surface, he'll get a definite feedback that he will associate with your displeasure as you give him a verbal rebuff and move in to flip your fingers against the offending foot and place it back in position. It's amazing how quickly this simple device can help to teach an obedient dog not to shift his feet on the **Stand.**

Although the work described above for stabilizing a dog and correcting the foot-shifting will be done separately from the Stand in Motion patterns, the effects will carry over to the formal exercise.

Work him on the light line until he's past contention on all parts of the exercise.

AKC REGULATIONS FOR
THE MOVING STAND AND EXAMINATION

Section 11. **Moving Stand and Examination.** The principal features of the exercise are that the dog heel, stand and stay on command by the moving handler, accept the examination without shyness or resentment, and, on command, return to the handler.

Orders for the exercise are "Forward," "Stand your dog," given while the handler is walking, "About Turn," "Halt," and "Call your dog to heel."

The handler stands with his dog sitting in the heel position at a point indicated by the Judge. The Judge asks "Are you ready?" and orders "Forward." The handler commands or signals his dog to heel, and walks briskly at a normal pace. After the handler has proceeded about 10 feet the Judge orders

"Stand your dog." The handler, without pausing, commands and/or signals the dog to stand, continues forward 10–12 feet and, on order of the Judge, turns to face his dog and halts. The dog must stand and stay in position.

The Judge approaches the dog from the front and examines the dog by going over it with his hands as in dog show judging except that in no circumstances shall the examination include the dog's mouth or testicles.

The Judge then orders "Call your dog to heel," whereupon the handler commands and/or signals the dog to return to the heel position. The dog immediately returns in a brisk manner to the proper heel position beside the handler.

Section 12. **Moving Stand and Examination, Scoring.** A score of zero is required for the following: A dog displaying fear or resentment, moving from the place where it was left, sitting or lying down before being called, growling or snapping at any time during the exercise, repeated whining or barking, the dog's failure to heel, stand and stay, accept the Judge's examination, or return to the handler.

Substantial to minor deductions, depending on the circumstances, must be made for a dog that moves his feet repeatedly while remaining in place.

All appropriate penalties of the Novice Heel Free, Stand for Examination and Recall exercises shall apply. Minor or substantial penalties, depending on extent, shall be made for the handler that changes the manner of walking or hesitates or pauses while giving the command and/or signal to stand, or if the dog fails to return briskly or sit properly in the heel position.

Half the dowel's length is concealed but the scent is the same.

6

The Directed Jump

$\mathbf{A}$ STUDY of the American Kennel Club's description of the Directed Jump will remind you that there are about twelve actions that a dog must take to successfully perform the exercise.

1. He must sit in the **Heel** position, attentive to his handler until sent on the **Go out.**
2. When commanded to do so, he must go at a brisk pace toward the other end of the ring.
3. Upon receiving a command, he must turn and sit with his attention on the handler.
4. He must execute the jump which the handler indicates.
5. After jumping, he must angle in to a sit-position in front of the handler.
6. He must **Finish** on command.

The dog must then repeat the six steps in relation to the second jump, making a total of twelve demands for specific acts of obedience. Three of these acts are new to the dog: the **Go out,** the **Turn and Sit,** and the response to the command and signal that indicates the Judge's choice of a jump.

To deal with the complexity of the exercise, we will work on each of the components as a separate entity, and combine them after they have all been mastered.

THE GO OUT

In the logical order of progression, we'll begin with the **Go out** component. Our task will be one of **positive motivation,** more than teaching. If you have a positive retriever who knows he must retrieve instead of a natural, play-the-game retriever who retrieves when there is nothing else he would sooner do, we can motivate him in such a way that he'll run toward the far end of the ring until you command him to turn and sit facing you. This fact will cheer you if you are one of those who are nauseated by the sight of a dog who tentatively oozes away from his handler with backward glances, then "buttonhooks" such a short distance beyond the jumps that a clean execution of either jump is impossible. You'll have something stronger going for you than tidbits, pulleys, playthings, or a person who has bribed the dog by sitting strategically at the far end of the ring with a lunchbox. The motivation found most effective is that of the **Blind Retrieve.** The strength of this reasonable technique was fully explained in Chapter Four.

Level 1—Objective: To reliably find and retrieve a dowel from cover over a distance of six feet.

Find a discarded handle from a broom or mop and cut five six-inch lengths from it. If no handle is available, obtain a piece of dowling of similar size from a hardware store or lumber yard.

Only if your dog is one of the Toy breeds should you go to a smaller diameter dowel—and in fairness to the little guy, nothing smaller than one-half inch in diameter.

Whether most of your trials will be held on lawn, floor, or pavement, there will be some advantages in starting this component on grass. The work of the first week need not be in a ring environment.

Obtain enough long grass or other cover such as straw or leaves to make a cover two feet long, a foot wide, and a few inches deep. Do not let another person handle your dowels or the cover material lest his scent cause later complications. Arrange your covering material before you bring the dog to the area. Put one dowel in your pocket. Take your dog at **Heel** to the work area. It is assumed that your dog is trained in Open work and is force-broken to retrieve, in which case you are fully qualified to use the following method with little difficulty. Conversely, the handler of a make-a-game retriever won't have as much leverage to insure the dog's cooperation. However, even in the second instance, he would still have a more logical approach than if he were using the pulley or lunchbox.

First of all, familiarize your dog with the dowel by having him hold it a few times.

Next, have him retrieve it, a leash length, several times. Now put him on a **Sit-Stay** facing your cover arrangement from a leash length distance. Put the dowel on top of the approximate center of the cover; and return to position beside your dog. Give your usual verbal command, and include the word **Go.** Such as: "Joe, **Go** fetch," or "Joe, **Go,** take it." **Later at the right time, only the word "Go," in combination with his name, will be used to send him out.** Reward his good performance with lots of praise for retrieving an object that was placed, not thrown. If he failed to retrieve, correct him as you did for such disobedience in your Open training. You introduced him to the dowel fairly. It would defeat your purpose of reliable motivation to give him a second command, or to let him scramble to retrieve just ahead of the correction his poor response had earned.

Again, it is assumed that you had trained your dog to retrieve reliably before you started Utility training and it is believed that you know how to correct effectively for any failure to fetch.

Have your dog make two more retrieves, each time placing the dowel and handling the dog as you did in the first instance.

Next, place the dowel in the same place but conceal about

half of its length with a bit of the cover. Send the dog. If he's at least a fair retriever, he won't be confused by the partial concealment of the dowel. The scent hasn't changed; and he's got a nose. Be strong in your praise for a good job, and strong in correcting for any failure. Have him retrieve the partially hidden dowel two more times.

Place the dowel in exactly the same place. Cover it lightly, but completely. Send the dog. Because you prepared for the moment as described above, the dog should go to the cover, locate the dowel by scent, and paw or root it out so he can make the retrieve.

Add a lot of praise to his feeling of success.

Be ready to correct for any failure which could come in one of several ways:

1. The dog could fail to move out when he doesn't see the dowel.
2. He could go to the cover and make a token effort to sight the object on top of, or near, the pile, and then finally quit working.
3. He might definitely locate the dowel by scent but make no effort to root it out.

In case of any of these failures, your correction should convince him that the same abilities he would use to find and uncover something he wants to find must be used to find and uncover something *you* want, even when he doesn't want to do it. He'll soon show you he'd rather root the dowel clear of its cover than have to grab it along with a mouthful of grass in a hurried response to correction. There is absolutely no kindness in being charitable to confusion at this level; it would only postpone the reckoning to a less favorable time. Also, the reasons you should not try to bridge any gaps by substituting food or toys for the dowel will soon be apparent to you.

The probability that he will get some of the cover material in his mouth is no reason for him to refuse to pick up the dowel nor for you to excuse him. It is said that a dog in Elroy, Illinois, actually ate some grass. So?

Even when the dowel is completely covered, the dog should locate it by scent and root it from cover.

Hang in there until your dog locates, uncovers, and retrieves the dowel you conceal.

Work until your dog has made three consecutive **Blind Retrieves** of the dowel, then end the session. Give him a little time to himself before you start work on another component of the **Signal exercise.**

Each day for a week, whether you work one long period or two short ones, require your dog to make a half-dozen consecutive **Blind Retrieves.** By the end of that time, he will have enjoyed a lot of success and praise, and will be ready to start the next level.

Level 2—Objective: To make the dog aware of three facts.

1. Even though he does not see a dowel placed, he must go on your command, find and retrieve.
2. He must retrieve over increased distances.
3. If sent, he must go out for a second concealed object because there could be more than one.

First day

Put two dowels in your pocket. Attach a longe line, such as pictured on page 17, to the dog's collar, and head for your pile of cover. While the dog holds a **Sit-Stay** in the familiar place, put the dowels about a foot apart on top of the cover. At this time, it is unimportant whether or not the dog sees you place them.

Return to the dog and send him. It makes no difference which of the dowels he retrieves first or whether he brings them back together: praise him for the retrieve. Do not permit any indecision to prevent him from retrieving.

If he goes back and forth from one dowel to another without picking up either, correct him to one of them. When he's brought back one dowel, send him for the other. **If he brought back the two together, he has still made two pickups**

and has learned that there might be more than one object for him to find and fetch.

Work the dog in the same pattern until he has retrieved the two dowels without contention three times in a row.

Now that he's had this experience in consecutive retrieves when the dowels are in plain sight, it's time to cover one of them lightly. Send the dog as before. He'll probably retrieve the visible dowel first. However, an occasional dog is so scent-oriented that he'll root out and retrieve the hidden object first. Whether your dog finds by sight or by scent, praise him for the retrieve and send him for the second dowel. Repeat the "one sighted, one scented" retrieving order until the dog performs it proficiently. This is a good place to end work on this component for the period.

Second day

It's time to give your dog practice in going out to retrieve when neither dowel is in sight, in preparation for the time when there will be no cover or any other sight to direct him until after he has moved out on your command. The routine of placing the dowels and handling the dog is exactly the same except that you lightly cover both dowels. Send him. Familiarity with the pattern and the sight of the cover will direct him to the pile.

The experience he's had in scenting and rooting out the objects will help him to speedily find a dowel. As soon as you've praised him for retrieving the first dowel, send him for the second. Don't accept any slow starts or dallying. **Make him solid while you are close to him: don't postpone a confrontation until distance gives him the physical advantage.** Be equally prompt and emphatic with praise for his good performance.

Work until he has done the double **Blind Retrieve** three times without contention, which will indicate that he's accepted two facts:

It makes no difference which of the two dowels the dog retrieves first.

1. He must **Go out** when he's told to fetch, whether or not he sees what he should retrieve.
2. He can locate the objects by scent as well as by sight.

Stop work at this high point and give him a break—a quiet break, not a play break, before you go to another component.

Third day

Your dog has demonstrated that he's ready to begin **Blind Retrieving** over greater distances. Work him on a couple of patterns just as you did the previous day. On about the third set-up, work with your longe, so you can move back two feet farther, which would be approximately eight feet. Although the cover is still there for a focal point, he'll get some practice in traveling a bit farther to retrieve.

There are a few con-artist dogs that will try a trainer in what they would like to claim is a new situation.

When your dog is successful at the eight-foot distance, add another two feet to the length of the retrieve. Work until he's done three consecutive ten-foot retrieves of both dowels without contention.

Fourth day

Repeat the work of the third day so that your dog will have a bit more practice in **Blind Retrieving** two objects over a distance of ten feet, which was the objective for that day. Set a distraction off to one side, but far enough so that avoidance won't cause the dog to go to the cover indirectly. The extra practice will pay off in quick starts on a straight line as we leave the pile of cover and begin work in an actual ring environment.

Level 3—Objective: To **Blind Retrieve** two dowels from a ten foot distance in a ring environment.

First day

Many problems, which can be avoided by a careful, step-by-step procedure, will plague a student-trainer who so occupies himself with "yeah, buts" that he closes his mind to the very continuity that would supply the answers to his valid questions.

Your best understanding of the progression used for beginning a dog's **Go out** in the ring environment will come from a step-by-step walk-through and holding to the work patterns when they're understood.

Set up a ring as shown on page 19.

Arrange the dowels before you bring the dog to the area. Put one dowel on the centerline of the ring about six feet past the jump line and a second dowel about a foot beyond the first. You've been working with the leash and longe but now is a good time to familiarize yourself and the dog with the seventy-foot check-cord. Although far lighter than the longe, the check-cord is practically unbreakable. Nylon can be used, but almost all trainers prefer other materials that give a better grip and are not as likely to cause a burn.

Lay the snap of the cord on the centerline **between the jumps,** with about twenty feet of it lying loose from the coil so that it will slide freely through the grass, and so, if necessary, you'll have grabbing room.

Bring your dog to the area. Fasten the cord to his collar, or, if you anticipate the need of a good handle, to his tab. Take a position facing the dowels so that your dog is seated on the **center point between the jumps.**

Gradually, he will become accustomed to the peripheral presence of the jumps and will understand that he is to go between them on the way out.

Send the dog. It's a new location. **The dog will not see the dowel from his eye level—even if the grass is short.** Regardless of these complications, he should start out when you

From the dog's height and location, the dowels cannot be seen.

send him. Rejoice and be exceedingly glad that you gave him all that practice retrieving the dowels from cover. What you ask is reasonable. Lo and behold, as he goes straight away from you in the pattern your work has instilled, the dowels will come into his sight. Again, it makes no difference which dowel he retrieves first. Heap a lot of praise on him for the first **Go out** in the ring environment. The strong foundation you've given him would certainly justify a tough correction if he fails to respond to your first command.

This is a critical moment. Remember—the only command permitted in the ring is the first one. Don't be one of those weird handlers who give the second command, kitchy-coo, or trot out to the dowels as an enthusiastic example for a dog. **Come D-Day you won't be able to chortle and trot.**

Immediately after you've praised the dog for the first retrieve, send him for the second dowel. Give him a few more experiences, and a break, before you go to the next component.

Second through sixth days

Don't be tempted by your dog's good performance to extend the pattern too rapidly. You will gain nothing by pressing too hard on one component, only to mark time while other parts of the exercise are brought up to the same level. You will gain much in giving your dog lots of practice in a prompt response and concentration; and yourself practice in sending him out confidently.

Competence and confidence are particularly interactive in the Obedience ring. As mentioned before, diligently study the Regulations. They permit you a choice of commanding your dog to **Go** with or without a signal. Most handlers recognize an advantage in using both. Studying the handling form of the better exhibitors in your area should help you to polish your own style.

By the end of the week, both you and your dog should be working smoothly on the ten foot **Go out.**

Level 4—Objective: Extend retrieve pattern to fifteen feet.

First day

Work a couple of review patterns exactly like those of the previous day. Review finished, extend the pattern. Place the dowels only a few inches farther down the ring from their previous positions. Bring your dog to a starting point about two feet behind the crossline of the jumps. His previous experience in starting from the crossline has accustomed your dog to the peripheral presence of the jumps, so now he should feel no reason to try to jump on the way out, as he did in Open work.

Give him four experiences in retrieving the dowels.

Second day

By now your dog has a strong association with the word **Go,** and you can reasonably eliminate **Fetch** or **Take it** from your command. If you've been adding an and/or signal, you may continue to do so.

Third day

Place the dowels a foot farther down ring than previously, and send the dog from a foot farther back. This spacing should total, roughly, about fifteen feet. It is unlikely that such a short move back from the jumps will cause your dog to feel he should go over one of them as he goes out; but, if he starts to do so, snub him up with your cord and make a correction that takes him straight down the centerline to where he can grab a dowel. He should hold it while you back-pedal, towing him back to where the retrieve started, **and where it should finish,** so he can sit in front of you and you can take the dowel from him in the usual manner.

Fourth and fifth days

Use exactly the same pattern as on the third day. Rarely does a dog need more than five days of experience at this level to reach the objective of fifteen-foot blind retrieves, but if you feel your dog needs it, give him an extra day or two.

Level 5—Objective: To extend retrieve pattern to twenty feet.

First day

Move your dog's starting point one foot back from the previous position and place the dowels a foot farther down ring than before. Give the dog three experiences in retrieving the two dowels at this distance.

Second through fifth days

Lengthen the pattern a bit each day so that by the fifth day your dog is going from five feet behind the crossline to retrieve the dowels from a point about fifteen feet down ring.

Level 6—Objective: To add a third dowel to the pattern and extend distance to thirty feet.

First day

Place a dowel about fifteen feet out from the crossline and align the others at one foot intervals beyond it. Bring your dog to the same spot from where you've been sending him and attach your check-cord. As previously stated, the check-cord is a necessity.

Your dog will drag a line through the heaviest grass if he is a positive retriever—**because he knows he must.** When he's dragging a line, he knows that he cannot run to avoid a correction that he might possibly deserve. It will also enable you

"Apple" is now going out farther than would ever be required in an obedience trial.

to snub him up if he tries to go out over a jump instead of down the centerline. Furthermore, the line will be needed when you work on other components. Give him at least three consecutive experiences in retrieving the set of three dowels. Praise him warmly for each good performance—and at the right time, which is when he brings a dowel to you, not after he does the finish.

If, as he goes out, he should be distracted by a scent or an unusual sight, grab the cord to stop him from scrambling to a dowel to avoid the correction his delay earned, work your way to him, and correct him all the way to a dowel. **Don't intersperse his goof and your correction with a nice walk back to the dowel.**

Second day

The dowels should be placed approximately two feet farther down-ring than previously, and the dog should be sent from two feet farther back from the crossline, which adds up to about twenty-four-foot retrieves. Other than this, the pattern of work is the same as on the first day.

Third through fifth days

Each day, lengthen the distance between the dowels so that by the end of the fifth day the dog is going from a position ten feet behind the jump line to retrieve dowels the closest of which is twenty feet beyond the jumps.

Level 7—Objective: To retrieve four dowels over a fifty foot distance.

First day

Work the dog in a review of the previous level's pattern a couple of times. Next, place the three dowels as before and align a fourth dowel a foot beyond them. Give your dog two experiences in retrieving the four dowels. Be enthusiastic in your praise when it's deserved and consistent when corrections are needed. Your dog will become increasingly convinced that **he must go as many times as you send him because there is always a dowel,** if needed, to make corrections possible.

Second through seventh days

During the next six days you should be able to gradually lengthen the retrieves until your dog is going out from twenty feet behind the jump line to get dowels from at least thirty feet beyond the jumps.

Level 8—Objective: To extend pattern to seventy feet.

First through seventh days

"But why train a dog to go out seventy feet when the average ring is not even that long?"

The answer is twofold. First, by conditioning him to go out well past the point where you would be likely to turn and sit him in the ring, you will make sure that he will go out purposefully and straight: like he's going out to do something. How much better than if he were to ooze a few feet out between the jumps and "buttonhook" around to sit off-center in no position to execute one of the jumps which you can bet, is the jump any judge would indicate. Second, the effort needed to make the long **Blind Retrieves** will stimulate his hunting instincts and bring a surprising buoyancy to his performance. Contrary to what most experimental psychologists would believe, the dog who is forced to accept this responsibility increases in enthusiasm. This hard drive will enable you to turn and sit your dog when he has reached a favorable spot down ring. Without that drive, your job would be more difficult. So work confidently and you'll win out.

Blind Retrieving the dowels causes a dog to go out straight and buoyantly.

Very gradually make adjustments so that by the end of the week you will be able to stand twenty feet behind the jump line and send your dog to retrieve the four dowels, the farthest of which will be at least fifty feet beyond the jumps.

As stated above, I am aware that the lengths of these retrieves would take him from where he's sent right out of the end of the average ring. No, he won't form a bad habit of going beyond the ring rope. If you've been training in a ring set-up, as you should have been, move the end rope back to accommodate the lengthened retrieves.

Though the action is the same, the longer retrieves will subject your dog to more smells and other distractions, and the feel of remoteness might encourage him to goof. If such is the case, snug up the line so he can't make that last second lunge to grab a dowel ahead of your correction, and work your way, hand over hand and correct him to the dowel in your usual way. **Remember, you can't move to threaten him in a trial, so you must convince him that "any wait will be too late" in training.**

When your dog goes out solidly to retrieve the set of four dowels two consecutive times, a total of eight retrieves without contention, you will be prepared to begin the delicate task of adding the **Turn and Sit** to the **Go out.**

TURN AND SIT COMPONENT

Level 1—Objective: To sit from a standing position at a leash length from trainer.

First through seventh days

Take your dog, on leash, to a point on the centerline of the ring about twenty feet past the jumps. Place him on a **Stand-Stay** facing toward the jump line. This is the approximate spot from where he will see your signal and the jumps when later he performs the complete exercise. He could gain a little something from seeing the jumps from the same distance all through

Prevent your dog from getting the habit of inching forward by giving him a week of work on sitting from a stand a leash length away from you.

much of his work on the **Turn and Sit** component. Face him from one long step away.

After a few seconds, give the command: "Joe, **Sit.**" He knows what **Sit** means, so if he hesitates, step in and enforce a response. When he sits in the spot where he received the command, praise him and circle around him to end the pattern as though you were finishing a **Sit-Stay.**

Your dog will learn this simple step from just a few experiences, but he will gain much from his success and your praise if you will give him ten such experiences each day for a week. He should then be sitting promptly with no sign of contention.

Level 2—Objective: To turn toward the trainer and sit.

First through seventh days

Place your dog on a **Stand-Stay.** Move to a position about four feet behind him. Command, "Joe, **Sit,**" and in the same instant use the leash to turn him around toward you and sit him. Do not let him come toward you more than he would be honestly required by the turn: if need be, step in and square him up properly. Work him ten times every day on this pattern. It should be possible for you to move back a few inches farther behind him each day, but do not extend the pattern so fast that you would be unable to prevent slow responses or sloppy patterns from forming. Later, much later, you will need to turn and sit him on command when he is on the **Go out;** it would be more difficult to correct bad habits as the distance increases and the components are being brought together.

By the end of a week your dog should turn from a **Stand** and **Sit** facing you from a leash length away, with only a command from you.

After the first week, it should be time to turn your dog and sit him.

Level 3—Objective: To extend the **Turn and Sit** pattern to ten feet.

First through seventh days

The handling of a dog on the **Turn and Sit** requires a bit more care and skill as the distance is increased. This is particularly true because you will need to use something longer than your more comfortable leather leash. Use your check cord.

Give your dog some practice at the distances achieved at the last level. When he's working smoothly, lengthen the distance between you a foot. Each day, move back gradually when it seems reasonable to do so, but do not stand more than ten feet in back of the dog by the end of the week. **Remember, it is when you are still close to the dog that you can set good patterns by moving in swiftly to correct faults.**

When your dog seems to be past the point of contention while working at the above distance from you, it will be reasonable to begin the next level.

Level 4—Objective: To extend the **Turn and Sit** pattern to twenty-five feet.

First through tenth days

Work your dog in a few patterns at the ten-foot distance, then, as his smooth performance warrants, begin to lengthen your working distance a few inches at a time. Work him about ten times each day, preferably during more than one period. **Do some of your work around distractions, so that he'll know you'll accept no excuse for inattentiveness.** Normally, it takes about twenty days of working the dog faithfully to lengthen the distance to where a trainer can stand twenty-five feet behind his dog and cause him to turn and sit reliably regardless of distractions; however, even if it should take you longer, be certain that your dog will turn and sit on command without the slightest second cue before you attempt the next level.

Gradually lengthen the distance until he will turn and sit infallibly at least fifty feet from you.

Level 5—Objective: Extend **Turn and Sit** pattern to full working distance.

Begin work by doing a few review practice patterns at the previous maximum distance. Increase your working distance when you feel it is reasonable to do so, but no more than a foot each day. Regardless of how well your dog works, be prepared to make an occasional correction. Corrections for place and position should be made as consistently as they were at closer distances. Don't nag your dog into neurosis. Pop it to him with finality.

The praise you give for each good response should tell him he's the world's greatest dog, but it should not release him from his duty to hold his position. "Waiting for you to follow the judge's instruction" will be a very important factor in the performance of the **Directed Jump exercise.** After you give him a word of praise for turning and sitting, look off obliquely, so you won't appear to be bearing down as you walk toward him. Give him more praise for holding the **Sit** position until you end the pattern. If he should lie down from confusion, or for any other reason, as you return, grab the cord and remind him that the command was to **Sit.**

From this point on, progress in lengthening your working distance will depend on the foundation you've built, and ability—yours and your dog's. Records on the author's Utility classes indicate that one should expect any properly worked dog to turn and sit on command from a stand at a distance of fifty feet after eight weeks of training on the exercise, which is the stage at which all components can be combined in the **Directed Jump exercise.**

The time increments allotted to the various levels of this exercise are approximations based on wide experience and should help provide a perspective to the reader, who will realize that the learning abilities of dogs will vary. **Regardless of time required, be certain that your dog is past contention at the fifty-foot distance before you try to combine this component with the other parts of the exercise.**

Regardless of how reliably your dog responds, do not shorten the cord until after the components are combined.

Sandbag or otherwise anchor your jumps so they will be stable. The fine wire laced between the standards will prevent a dog from going under the bar.

SIGNAL AND JUMP

Level 1—Objective: Basic patterns in response to command and signal.

Here is the "how" and "why" of preparing your jumps as you begin work on the **Signal and Jump** component. First of all, even though you will be working with small patterns at the start, there will be a slight advantage in spacing the jumps according to the regulations, which are: ". . . midway in the ring at right angles to the sides of the ring and eighteen to twenty feet apart, the bar jump on one side, the high jump on the other."

Sandbag or otherwise anchor the jumps so they will be stable if bumped. Place the bar on the side of the standards from which your dog will be jumping so that the drag of a line won't dislodge it, which is the opposite of the way it would be in a trial. Notice how the easily attached, heavy rubber bands are looped around the standard, bar and pin to make the bar even more secure. Although your dog has been jumping the regulation height in Open work, set both the jumps at such a low level that **over** instead of **under** is the only logical way for your dog to negotiate the bar. The lacing of hardly visible black wire, as shown on page 118, will block the space from ground to bar.

Position yourself and your dog in relation to the high jump as shown on page 123. Accustoming your dog to an angled approach is important because ultimately he will run from where he has sat on the **Go out** to the indicated jump at about a thirty degree angle. In these early stages, you will be the focus for that angle. Study the position carefully. Notice how the leash is held in the left hand to accommodate the dog's position to your left.

Command, "Joe, **Over,**" and simultaneously throw your arm out as shown, and run hard at an angle that will bring the dog over the center of the jump. Yes, run hard although you are sure he would jump without any movement on your part; for, until you are told to do differently, you should make it absolutely necessary for him to follow the angle of that leash.

Tying the signal and the significance of the alignment into the pattern at a point where the demands are so obvious and simple is both effective and kind to the dog. As the feel of the leash tells you he's clearing the jump, call back a hearty word of praise. Pivot to face him right where you are, and bring him in to sit in front of you. End the pattern with your usual **Finish.**

The foregoing is an easy pattern that your dog will enjoy, so give him a few more experiences on the familiar solid jump before you switch to the bar jump.

The placing of your dog and yourself for executing the bar jump on your left will employ the same principles as were applied when you worked on the high jump. Obviously, you will hold the leash in the right hand as you signal with the left. It is unlikely that your dog will balk at jumping the bar when it is placed so low. The lacing beneath it leaves one practical route—over the top. Praise, pivot to bring the dog to sit before you, and finish the action as you did in the experience with the high jump. After a few jumps, the standard and bar will mean **Over** as graphically as does the high jump.

When practicing either jump, it is important to position yourself and dog so that the angle is correct and there is slack in the leash. If your dog takes your positioning and arranging of the leash as a cue to move before your command, correct him back the way he came. Any dog in advanced training should hold a **Sit-Stay.**

Be sure to coordinate your verbal command and signal, by considering Regulations, yet giving every possible advantage to your dog. According to the Regulations, a handler may indicate the selected jump for the dog with a "command and/or signal."

There are advantages in using both the command and signal. The name and a verbal command is an attention-getter should the dog not be looking, and the signal indicates a direction better than a word could. A good handler calls the name, and then starts his arm movements a trifle before the word of command, so that, if the dog should anticipate, he will do so in the right direction. To give an arm signal after the dog has headed for a jump is a futile gesture. Practice giving a clean, properly timed command and signal so that maximum clarity will be natural to your later handling in the ring. Have someone watch to see that you are precise in your handling. Even a major league pitcher slips out of form occasionally, and needs a coach to watch his motion.

Your arm should extend out from the shoulder as far as possible and the dog should get a full view of your open hand. Turn and run the instant you give the signal and command. It's too early to trust his initiative. Run. If he fails to start and gets snubbed into the jump, he'll learn that a quick jump in the right direction is the best policy. That rapidly moving leash leaves no time for contention.

Hitting a jump will not cause him to suffer a "trauma" unless you tell him he's had a terrible experience by commiserating with him.

Continue to give that word of praise as he clears a jump, and pivot cleanly so that he gets practice in sitting in front of you.

Work your dog four or five times on each jump every day, carefully observing the above principles. He should be executing the jumps reliably and happily by the end of the week. Then you and your dog will be prepared to begin a program of extending those patterns toward the time when you will be standing on the centerline of the ring and your dog will sit facing you on that same line from more than forty feet away.

Level 2—Objective: Extending patterns to regulation distance.

Dogs vary in the time it takes them to become solid on the **Directed Jump exercise,** so at best one can only set a reasonable and flexible schedule of progress; and outline the "where" and "why" of the major changes in pattern. The pictures and comments that follow should be a useful aid to that progress. Above all, be honest in your judgment of when your dog is past contention on one step and ready for the next.

COMBINING THE COMPONENTS

You taught the **Directed Jump** components separately so each was a complete, understandable task in itself and so that your praise and corrections could be given with the utmost clarity. Your dog has learned to perform each component precisely and dependably. Combine the components as carefully as you taught them. The following progressions will help you put it all together in a logical and positive way for you and your dog.

Level 1—Objective: To combine the Go out with the Turn and Sit.

First through twelfth days

The delicate process of turning and sitting a dog on a **Go out,** before he gets to a dowel, must be done carefully so that he does not feel rebuffed when you abort his effort to retrieve. You must make no mistake in handling. Read and understand the logic of each step. **Walk through** the entire process, as much as possible, without the dog.

As always, leave your dog on a **Stay** from where he can not see you place the dowels. If you're a "yeah-but'r," roll the following truth around in your mind a bit. **Even a minute before you're due in the ring, at a licensed trial, you can:**

1. Show him a dowel or two.
2. Leave him on a stay where he can not see the ring.
3. Walk out of his sight and give the dowels to someone to hold for you.
4. Return to the dog and head for the ring.

Your dog couldn't know what you did with the dowels any more than a human could and the little ritual will remind him that there was always a dowel in place when he refused to go out.

You can see from this that the "leverage" you develop now in your training will be present later in the ring.

Study the text carefully so you will understand the reasons for the starting positions and actions in this and the next four photographs.

Now the handler and dog are ready to start closer to the inside standard.

123

The dog has learned to obey the signal even when not in line with the jump.

The starting positions are now back from the jump and close to the centerline.

125

Place the dowels as you did for the last pattern. Put the snap of your check-cord on the centerline about twenty-five feet past the jumps and lay its length back to the exact spot from where you will send the dog—which Regulations say should be "about twenty feet from the line of the jumps." Tie a knot in the cord as a marker. Let the cord lie on the ground, but be doubly careful to arrange it so that the knot won't snag on your foot and jerk the dog up short of a dowel.

We're not ready to check him until he's made a retrieve, and never with a jerk.

Send the dog for a dowel. Give him lots of praise for that first retrieve.

Now it's **D-Day.** Again, mentally walk through the following instructions before you use them. Sit your dog on the sending spot. Once more, check your line to see that it won't foul on you or your dog. Grip the line with your right hand at the marker knot. Send your dog. Just before your approximately forty-five feet of slack is about to tighten, command, "Joe, **Sit.**" Take a step forward to cushion any shock as you apply a firm but gradual restraint that stops his forward progress and turns him so that he will sit facing you from about five feet from where you started to check him, which will be about twenty-five feet past the jumps, and about fifteen feet short of the first dowel. Your cushioned restraint will stop and turn him, but it cannot enforce your sit command. Although you have worked him on turning and sitting at a distance as a separate component, he could be honestly confused by getting a command to do so while he's in motion. If he fails to sit, quickly give the second command with emphasis. There is nothing inconsistent about a second command at the start of this unusual situation. It simply tells him that he heard you correctly while he's learning to put things together.

The moment he sits, praise him; then move toward him, looking off obliquely so you won't give the appearance of bearing down to correct him. Walk around behind him to his right side as though you were returning on the **Sit-Stay** exercise. This action will help to condition him to wait for direction on that component where you will signal him to jump. Praise him for the "waiting."

The handler doesn't run, but the dog obeys the signal so he won't be trapped by the prearranged line.

Now it's D-Day! This is no time for poor handling.

Bring him back to the starting point in a relaxed manner. Make him feel with your attitude and action that he has done a good thing. Even if he turned and sat in perfect relation to the jumps, it would have been a poor time to do the **Signal and Jump.** He should feel the **Turn and Sit** component a bit more before it is blended into another action.

Square him up, arrange your line, and send him again. This time do not stop and sit him. If for any reason, such as anticipation of a stop or distractions, he should fail to retrieve, correct him from where he goofed all the way to the closest dowel. **This is your way to show him that he must always go out to make a retrieve unless you command him to turn and sit.**

If you have to correct, work until he makes a willing retrieve before you turn him and sit him again, even if it means making another set up with the dowels. Praise him a lot when he gives you that good retrieve. Square him up for another **Go out** and arrange your line. Send him. **Turn and Sit** him. Give him some praise from a distance when he sits, and some more praise when you go out to him. If he should be confused and lie down in spite of your smooth approach, snatch him back up to a sit and praise him in that position. Take him back to the sending point.

By now if all went as it should have, your dog will have made two retrieves, and you will have turned and sat him twice. Two more dowels remain out on that centerline. Clear him by sending him out for them. **It is important that his last two experiences, in this area of practice, be unaborted retrieves.** If at any point a block develops and he dawdles on the way out, or seems to anticipate a command to **Turn and Sit,** work him on straight retrieves until he is going out purposefully again.

It's true that Obedience Regulations do not penalize a crooked **Turn and Sit** but the advantages of having a dog sit straight on the centerline, and deep enough to make for a shallow angle to either jump, are very important. That's why we want to smooth out the **Turn and Sit** before we add the remaining component.

Practice two full patterns as they are described above. To summarize the patterns order:

1. A clean retrieve.
2. Send the dog and **Turn and Sit** him.
3. A clean retrieve.
4. Send the dog and **Turn and Sit** him.
5. Clear the dog by having him retrieve the last two dowels, so that the final responsibility is that of retrieving.

Generally, twelve days of such experience will bring a dog to a point where he will go straight out on a **blind retrieve** unless he hears his name and the **Sit** command, at which time he will **Turn and Sit** before the check-cord tightens. However, be sure to give your dog all the practice he needs to make him solid on the **Go** and the **Turn and Sit** before you add the **Signal and Jump** component to the pattern.

Level 2—Objective: To do complete directed jump patterns on the check-cord.

Until the dog is past contention

Set the dowels as you did for the last session. Send the dog for a dowel, or more if you need to resolve à difficulty such as hesitancy or bad direction. Next, send him and sit him on the **favorable spot.** Walk out and praise him as you've been doing. Whether your fault or his, if his **Sit** was not where you wanted it, move him to that place. Leave him on a **Sit-Stay.**

Arrange your line for a **Directed Jump** on your way back to where you'll give your signals. Wait a few seconds before you **Jump** him. Your handling on the **Signal and Jump** will be the same as when you worked on that component separately. When he's been praised for executing the first jump, send him on another **Go** and let him get a dowel. Square him up and send him out again. Give your command for a **Turn and Sit.** Handle all details for executing the second jump as you did for the first one. Both jumps completed, clear the dog by having him get the last two dowels. Give him lots of praise for the retrieves and end the session with a break that tells him he has just completed a good job.

A dog that goes the wrong way on a jump signal can be corrected by a prearranged cord and stake, as shown.

Shorten the light line gradually as you become increasingly sure of your dog's reliability.

After the break and some time on another exercise, repeat the above work.

There are good reasons for holding to the foregoing pattern to combine all of the components of the **Directed Retrieve.** You are the best judge of how much work your dog should have each day and how fast he should progress, but, ordinarily, twenty days of two experiences each day brings the average dog to a point where he is going out straight, turning and sitting on command, and holding that position until he obeys the command and signal to jump.

Even when his reliable and accurate **Turn and Sit** tells you that it's no longer necessary to walk out to praise or adjust him, continue to use a light line and shorten it gradually as you become increasingly sure of his good performance.

Work on the above program until your dog is completely past contention. Then polish and practice the **Directed Jump** as described in Chapter 7.

AKC REGULATIONS FOR THE DIRECTED JUMP

Section 13. **Directed Jumping.** The principal features of this exercise are that the dog go away from the handler in the direction indicated, stop when commanded, jump as directed and return as in the Recall.

The orders are "Send your dog," "Bar" or "High," and "Finish."

The jumps shall be placed midway in the ring at right angles to the sides of the ring and 18 to 20 feet apart, the Bar Jump on one side, the High Jump on the other. The Judge must make certain that the jumps are set at the required height for each dog by following the procedure described in Retrieve over the High Jump.

The handler, from a position on the center line of the ring and about 20 feet from the line of the jumps, shall stand with his dog sitting in the Heel position and on order from the Judge shall command and/or signal his dog to go forward at a brisk trot or gallop to a point about 20 feet beyond the jumps and

Even when the line is very short, the bar should be placed on the down-ring side of the standards so the drag won't pull it off.

in the approximate center. When the dog has reached this point the handler shall give a command to Sit; the dog must stop and sit with his attention on the handler but need not sit squarely.

The Judge will designate which jump is to be taken first by the dog and shall order either "High" or "Bar" when designating either the High or Bar Jump. The handler shall command and/or signal the dog to return to him over the designated jump. While the dog is in midair the handler may turn so as to be facing the dog as it returns. The dog shall sit in front of the handler and, on order from the Judge, Finish as in the Novice Recall. The Judge will say "Exercise Finished" after the dog has returned to the Heel position.

When the dog is again sitting in the Heel position the Judge shall ask, "Are you ready?" before giving the order to send the dog for the second part of the exercise. The same procedure shall be followed for the second jump.

It is optional with the Judge which jump is taken first, but both jumps must be taken to complete the exercise and the Judge must not designate the jump until the dog is at the far end of the ring. The dog shall clear the jumps without touching them.

The height of the jumps shall be the same as required in the Open classes. The High Jump shall be the same as that used in the Open classes, and the Bar Jump shall consist of a bar between 2 and 2½ inches square with the four edges rounded sufficiently to remove any sharpness. The bar shall be painted a flat black and white in alternate sections of about 3 inches each. The bar shall be supported by two unconnected 4 foot upright posts about 5 feet apart. The bar shall be adjustable for each 2 inches of height from 8 inches to 36 inches, and the jump shall be so constructed and positioned that the bar can be knocked off without disturbing the uprights.

Section 14. **Directed Jumping, Scoring.** A dog must receive a score of zero for the following: anticipating the handler's command and/or signal to go out, not leaving the handler, not going out between the jumps, not stopping on command and remaining at least 10 feet beyond the jumps, anticipating the handler's command and/or signal to Jump, not jumping as directed, knocking the bar off the uprights, and climbing or using the top of the High Jump for aid in going over.

Substantial deductions shall be made for a dog that does not stop in the approximate center of the ring about 20 feet beyond the jumps, for a dog that turns, stops or sits before the handler's command to Sit and for a dog that fails to sit.

Substantial or minor deductions, depending on the extent, shall be made for slowness in going out or for touching the jumps, or for any display of hesitation or reluctance to jump. All of the penalties listed under Novice Recall shall also apply.

7

Practice and Polish

LONG AFTER trucks were in common use many veteran milk-wagon horses held their jobs because they "knew a route." They would angle across streets from curb to curb and make the right stops even while the man was rattling his way down the steps from a previous delivery. This ability to memorize the order of positions, sounds and sights is found in the highest degree in some dogs, as you would know if you ever tried to quietly open and close the action of a shotgun when an experienced hunting dog was in the house. A good coonhound will bawl his low opinion of you if you put your hip boots and spotlight in your car and delay in loading him. A motion picture dog of the unlimited "do it all" category will learn a routine to a cursed degree after a few takes, during which an "intelligent human" has blown his lines, and then begin to do his "bit" when he hears the sound of the "sticks" and the word "action." In such cases an "end slate" is often used so the dog doesn't sweep into the scene on a wave of adrenalin.

Our Utility dogs, by reason of the significant sensory experience they have gained through three levels of training, will often cue from the order of the exercises and other qualities of ring environment.

An educated dog's ability to memorize a routine poses a question: "Should I practice in Regulation order and in the pattern used in the ring or should I practice out of continuity and vary the pattern to prevent anticipation?"

Assuming that the question is coming from a person whose dog is proficient in all of the exercises, and that there are no particular problems to be solved, the answer is to practice the exercises in the order and patterns in which they will occur in the ring; and let the dog prepare himself mentally for the next exercise so that he is more aligned to the action. He will not be rigid to a pattern when you are using the exercises out of the ring environment. Let him be in a "comfortable continuity" when he's in a Utility ring environment. The judge cannot surprise you by changing the exercises in the ring.

The following suggestions on practicing the Utility work are based on the above philosophy.

Take advantage of your dog's sense of environment by practicing in a ring that meets the requirements described in the Utility Regulations that appear in this book. It is essential that you have a "judge" who through experience or careful pre-instruction is familiar with the order and form of the exercises and the manner and vocabulary he will use to give you direction. Have at least one "steward" to assist the "judge" in all of the ring procedures. Measuring jumps, and placing articles and gloves are all part of his job.

Don't have any more conversation with the "ring help" than you would if you were in an actual trial. Wear an arm band. Respond as though it's a real trial when the steward calls you into the ring, and position yourself in a formal way for the first exercise.

Should a problem develop during this first or subsequent sessions in the ring environment, it would be advisable to use your tab and a short piece of line until you've worked it out and the dog is past contention.

138

SIGNAL EXERCISE

The judge should work you in an average pattern: no more unless a need for a correction and a repetition develops. As soon as you finish the **Signal** work, take the position for the next exercise.

SCENT DISCRIMINATION

Follow the usual ring procedure of orienting the dog by letting him see the **wrong** articles being placed. The judge will ask you whether you want your first **right** one to be leather or metal. Stand with your back to the set-up while you rub up your **right** article and place it on the judge's work sheet.

Give your scent to the dog in the approved way. Whether or not you feel that this reminder of your scent is needed, the gesture is one more preliminary that will help to align the dog. When ordered to **send your dog,** turn and send him exactly as you would in a trial.

With no levity or other atmosphere other than ring formality, the judge should run you through the entire exercise. As he marks your score, give your praise and move with a cheerful anticipation into position for the next exercise.

DIRECTED RETRIEVE

What do you and your dog see as you stand with your backs to the unobstructed end of the ring? Without doubt the most impressive sight is that of the steward going past on his way to place the gloves behind you. This action is a strong sign to your dog that he is about to be sent on a **Directed Retrieve. Remember this vital fact.** The judge will indicate the glove by number. You will give the command to **Heel,** and turn in place, stopping so your dog faces the designated glove. You will then direct him to that glove. When the dog has completed his retrieve, the judge will indicate the exercise is finished.

MOVING STAND AND EXAMINATION

A good rule of thumb when polishing any obedience exercise is to make the mechanics of correction as similar as possible to the mechanics that you used to teach the exercise. This will make it easier for your dog to understand the correction.

The second rule of thumb is to get a lot of practice work in a proofing environment that will be more distracting than the dog would encounter under ring conditions. If you do enough of this, your dog will come to take a distraction, whether it occurs by chance or is staged, as a cue to be more attentive to you. Have the leash on when you use distractions that are strong enough to make the dog goof. Then use a light line or tab until he resists the strongest distractions.

If the problem is that he continues to move after you order him to stand while you continue walking, set up a distraction just off to the left of where you intend to stop him. If he turns his head away from you and continues to walk with you, pivot and bring your right hand around as you did when you taught the exercise, but so sharply that he's made uncomfortable by the hand that slaps against his chest. Because your mechanics are much the same as when you taught the exercise, your dog will realize his mistake. Your technique will allow your left hand to be free to pop him back up if he sits when you stop.

If he breaks the stand when you move away to face him, or when your "judge" approaches to examine him, go back swiftly and square up to correct him as described above.

One component of the exercise that can confuse a dog is when he is required to end the exercise by briskly returning to the **Heel** position on command. If he has a heavy pattern of sitting in front of you on the **Recall**, he might need more practice on-leash to let him know it's okay to skip the sit-in-front and go cheerfully to the **Heel** position where he'll get a lot of praise.

Even though he's eight or ten feet from you, do not use the **Recall** command. You must teach him to come the full distance and go directly to the **Heel** position when he hears the **Heel** command.

Your cast of practice judges should include varied types so that your dog will be prepared for the variety of judges who will approach him in the ring.

Read the rules carefully.

There is often a variation from one area of the country to another in the exact way judges interpret the rules for the newer exercises, and it is good to observe a few trials closely before you enter competition.

DIRECTED JUMP

Now concentrate! As you give your dog praise and turn to move into position for the next job, what is it that the two of you see? Yup! The steward is again going past you as he goes to gather the gloves. It's the same action that was a strong signal to your dog that he was going to be sent for a glove.

Even if he tried, the dog couldn't see whether the steward was carrying gloves. By the time you've gotten to where you turn and face him around for the **Directed Jump,** the steward has hurried back to his table. It's true that the dog will be positioned about "twenty feet from the line of the jumps" but he will be sent toward the same end of the ring as he was on the **Directed Retrieve.** This is why many dogs that have been worked on one glove after another in close sequence in practice have a tendency to angle off on the **Go out,** looking for a second glove, when they've seen the steward move out to pick up the gloves. Even though the handler's physical direction on the **Go out** might be somewhat different than he uses for the **Directed Retrieve,** the very graphic passing of the "glove person" influences many dogs to seek a second glove.

Fortunately, the method of **Blind Retrieving** by which you taught your dog to follow your direction is a good protection against the influence of the steward's actions. There's another little precaution that can help erase the glove from your dog's mind and square him mentally for the **Directed Jump.** Don't rush down to the point from where you will send the dog and whirl around to wait in place while the judge marks your last score. Use your own preliminary or "handle" to tell the dog that you'll be sending him straight out to where he has always gotten a dowel unless he has been stopped by the **Turn and Sit** component. There are many ways in which a sharp handler can tell a discerning dog that he is about to **Go out** or **Go way,** but not for a glove. The particular way in which you praise him for the last exercise before sending him can tell him much. It bears repeating that his experience on **Blind Retrieves** is your best insulation against confusion.

Add another important feature of your practice to the above influences. Follow the retrieve of the one glove by immediately having him **Go way** for the **Directed Jump** in your formal ring practice, and in sending him for a preplanted dowel when you must work alone. That's the way it will be in the ring. One glove then the **Directed Jump.**

Remember this fact when you send your dog: he will be at least forty feet away and traveling with his back to you when you give him the "Joe, **Sit,**" so use enough volume to carry over conflicting sounds.

Percentages favor a handler whose arm is extended in the **jump** signal a trifle before the dog hears the "Joe, **Over**" so that he doesn't start before he gets the direction.

BEFORE FORMAL TRIALS

By now you have practiced the Utility exercises individually in your training sessions and in routine order in your "polishing ring." You feel that your dog is working at his top form. However, increased entry fees and the rising cost of transportation to trials might encourage you to try your dog in a few nearby practice matches to see how he'll do in a strange and formal environment. Be careful! You could make a common mistake that would be humorous if it were not so costly. To enter an untried dog in a practice match where corrections are not allowed would give him a chance to learn that he could disobey you with impunity in the formal environment. Irrational as it is, there are still some individuals who go to these "no-correction" matches in the belief that by letting a dog practice his disobedience he will somehow become obedient.

Try your dog in a few correction matches where the cardinal fault would be a correction that was so inhibited as to be ineffective.

An example of the most helpful of these matches is the kind presented by the Los Perreros Dog Obedience Club of Pomona Valley, California. The rings, stewards and judges are as efficient and formal as those that would be found at a licensed trial. There is none of the levity that would tell a ring-wise dog that it's other than one of those "real shows" where he cannot be corrected.

When a dog goofs, the roof falls in; and he learns that "you can't always tell," and that it's better to play it safe. The surprised look on the face of one of these ring-wise dogs repays some of the entry fees he's blown.

You can lessen the chances of your dog becoming ring-wise by giving him experiences in a few of these realistic matches where he will give you an opportunity for a correction in the formal ring atmosphere.

Remember, without his seeing you, place some dowels before you bring him into the ring so you will be prepared in case you need to correct on the **Go out.** The dowels will not interfere with his performance of any other exercise.

What if a trainer lives in an area where there are none of these helpful matches? He should seek out other sensible trainers who realize that you don't rid a dog of his problems by letting him practice them, and organize some. Be sure to keep your matches as much as possible like an official trial. Publicize the service your group is offering, and you'll find that many trainers will thank you.

It takes a lot of time and effort to develop a reliable and high-scoring Utility dog. The foregoing suggestions on doing some of your correcting in a formal atmosphere can prevent the occurrence of some difficult problems.

Much success and happiness to you and your dog in the Utility ring and in all the other activities you share.